Walks in Ancient Wales

Robert Harris

Published by Sigma Leisure – an imprint of
Sigma Press, 5 Alton Road, Wilmslow, Cheshire SK9 5DY, England.

British Library Cataloguing in Publication Data
A CIP record for this book is available from the British Library.

ISBN: 978-1-85058-797-2 (13-digit); 1-85058-797-3 (10-digit)

Typesetting and Design: Sigma Press, Wilmslow, Cheshire.

Cover photographs: main picture – unnamed stone circle in the Rhinogs; bottom row, left to right – Pentre Ifan burial chamber, Moel Ty-uchaf stone circle, Maen-y-Bardd burial chamber *(all photographs by Robert Harris)*

Maps and illustrations: Robert Harris. Maps reproduced from Ordnance Survey mapping on behalf of The Controller of Her Majesty's Stationery Office. © Crown Copyright. Licence Number MC 100032058

Location map: PerroCarto, Machynlleth

Printed in Poland – Polskabook UK

Disclaimer: the information in this book is given in good faith and is believed to be correct at the time of publication. No responsibility is accepted by either the author or publisher for errors or omissions, or for any loss or injury howsoever caused. Only you can judge your own fitness, competence and experience.

Preface

This is a book of walks which visit the sites and monuments left to us by the prehistoric people of Wales. These people, in the late Neolithic and early Bronze Ages, were the first to settle and farm the land, and they were the first to build structures that still survive to this day. Their stone circles, standing stones and burial chambers can be found scattered throughout the beautiful Welsh countryside often linked together by ancient trackways that can still be followed.

The walks vary in length from as little as four miles to some of ten or more. Some follow quiet country lanes and footpaths down in the valleys beside our modern farms and villages, while others climb high into the still wild and remote mountains. Each walk visits sites that help us to understand more about the distant lives and customs of our ancestors, and often to follow the ancient paths and tracks that linked them.

Each walk is roughly circular, starting and finishing in a town or village that is easy to locate and convenient to reach by car. The walks pass through some of the most spectacular scenery in Wales and all are worthwhile in themselves, but I hope the historical element not only adds interest, but also gives a purpose and focus to each walk.

I have divided the book into three sections, Anglesey, North Wales and South Wales. Anglesey because of its physical separation from the mainland by the Menai Straits, and North and South Wales because their ancient populations were split, then as now, by the bleak and empty moorlands of central Wales.

When taking the higher level walks, always follow the usual rules of mountain safety. Go properly equipped, always carry a map and compass and know how to use them. Be prepared for sudden and dramatic changes in the weather. The maps in the books are sketch maps only. For greater accuracy and detail consult the appropriate O.S. Outdoor Leisure or Explorer sheet. The walks follow public rights of way, but some of the sites are on private land. Treat all the land with respect and, if in doubt, always ask permission. Equally importantly, respect these ancient and sacred sites, which in many cases have survived for over five thousand years. They are our link with our history and they reach out to us from the deep abyss of the past. Treat them with the respect they deserve and help to preserve them for future generations to appreciate.

Lastly I would like to express my gratitude to the following people, without whom the writing of this book would have been a much more difficult, and not nearly so enjoyable, an experience. Chris Starkie, Gren Clubley, Mike Scott and Rowenna for their company on many of the walks and Chris Scott for her hospitality. Mairi and Bethan for their invaluable proof reading and Sue Hughes and her family for their great help in translating the Welsh place names.

Bob Harris

Dedication
To my Mum, the central stone of my circle.

Contents

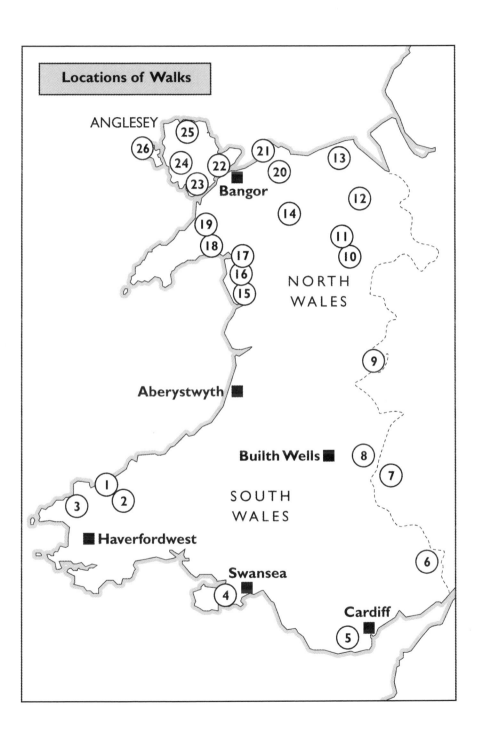

Locations of Walks

ANGLESEY

NORTH WALES

SOUTH WALES

Bangor

Aberystwyth

Builth Wells

Haverfordwest

Swansea

Cardiff

Key to symbols used on maps

❟	Standing Stone
⁞	Stone Circle
⁞	Cairn Circle
▬	Cairn or Tumulus
⁝	Ring Cairn
⁞	Enclosure or embankment
♠	Exposed Burial Chamber
◄	Longcairn
◄	Axe Factory
⌒	Cave
○	Hut Circle
♭	Spring or Well

Introduction

It was probably as long as 500,000 years ago that man first reached the land that we now know as Britain. They would have spread northwards from Europe, crossing what is now the English Channel, but was then open grassland stretching between low chalk hills. Ice would still have blanketed much of the land to the north, and the few scattered groups of people who ventured into this wilderness would have lived by hunting the herds of bison and reindeer that ranged over the mostly open landscape.

They would have sheltered in caves when they could find them but, more often, their homes would probably have been simple tents made of animal skins. We know that these early humans had broad flat noses and heavy jaws and they could make tools out of stone. They had also learnt how to make fire, which helped them to survive in the harsh conditions.

For hundreds of thousands of years, the weather fluctuated. At times, when it cooled, the ice would advance from the northern hills and the people would have retreated before it to the milder climate to the south. At other times the climate warmed, and man would have spread northwards, up the river valleys and along the coasts following the animals that they depended upon.

It is probable that, during just such a warm period, these early people would have first crossed over the Severn Valley into the lowlands of southern Wales.

These occupations would have been relatively short-lived, and for periods of thousands of years Britain would have been an icy wilderness devoid of all human life.

By about 60,000 years ago different humans, known as Neanderthals, had also spread northwards and were living in southern England and Wales. Sheltering in caves, these heavy boned people lived, like their earlier relatives, in small groups following and hunting the huge herds of deer and bison that ranged across the open tundra.

They were expert toolmakers, they could fashion warm clothes from animal skins and they had learnt to cook on their open fires. They cared for their sick and for the old and they buried their dead with simple, but symbolic ceremonies. They probably communicated with a well-developed speech and they were adaptable enough to have survived through the harsh weather of this bleak island.

They too, in their turn died out, but it was not because of the near arctic conditions or the advancing ice. Instead, it was the coming of modern man, Cro-Magnon man, which heralded the end of these early people.

These, our first direct ancestors, arrived about 40,000 years ago and it was relatively soon afterwards that the Neanderthals disappeared. Perhaps they were simply swamped by the sheer numbers of the newcomers and were absorbed into their developing society. Or perhaps they were forced out of their hunting grounds, pushed further and further into the arctic north, and were literally wiped out. Whatever the cause, from about 35,000 years ago to the present day, Britain has been inhabited by only one type of human, our ancestors!

For thousands of years, their numbers would have been relatively small, possibly no more than a few thousand people spread across the whole country. Then, about 12,000 BC, the land began to warm as the Ice Age finally ended. The glaciers retreated into the northern hills and the summers lengthened. The bare open slopes of the tundra sprouted with new life, and gradually, the land greened. Oak, willow and birch woodland spread over the valleys and coasts, and heather and grassland carpeted the lower hills.

With the trees came different animals, spreading northwards. Bears, wolves, deer, wild cattle and pigs flourished in the new forests and with them came people in ever-increasing numbers.

By about 6,000 BC the melting ice had caused the sea to rise sufficiently to cut Britain off from the continent. The rising temperatures had also allowed the hunters and gatherers of this Mesolithic period to spread to all but the most inhospitable northern mountains. Evidence, in the form of stone tools, has been found from this period from throughout Wales. Near the shores of the modern Llyn Brenig, a site has even been found where these people camped: a number of small fireplaces are surrounded by discarded flint tools and waste flakes. It is quite likely that a small travelling band stopped there for several nights as they hunted in the high and open heathlands above the wooded valleys.

They would probably have lived in groups of about thirty people, loosely linked by kinship. It is probable that the hunting parties would have been mostly young men, while the women and the children would have been responsible for the collecting of what fruit and nuts and roots were locally available. The old would have been supported and cared for, but would also have had their role within the group, possibly looking after the very young and the sick. They would have spoken a complex language, which would have allowed them to discuss and question and to express feelings. Their dead were honoured and buried with dignity.

Their lives would still have revolved around the animals they hunted,

Mesolithic microliths from North Wales

but the ever-spreading woodlands would have brought about a different way of life. No longer did the woodland animals have to travel vast distances in search of seasonal food, as did the great herds across the open tundra. They could stay and survive within the confines of the forest, moving to new grazing with ease. This allowed the hunters to stay within their own territories, within which they could hunt or collect all the food that they needed for their group.

From this stability would have come the beginnings of a sense of place, of belonging to an area and an understanding of it and an attachment to it. Their camps would still have moved through the year, up onto the moors in summer, down into the woods in winter – and they would have known where the fruit and berries could be found and at what times of the year.

As they settled into their territories, they would have begun, very gradually, to adapt and change the landscape around them. Paths would slowly form between seasonal camps and to water sources and trees were cleared to make room for their simple huts.

They would almost certainly have noticed that old clearings allowed the grasses to grow and that this better grazing attracted the animals on which they depended. From that, it was only a short step to actively clearing patches of woodland to entice their prey to where they could be killed more easily. They would have noticed that discarded seeds grew where they were dropped and that useful plants and trees could be encouraged to grow where they were most needed.

Over time, a social memory would slowly develop. Certain places would become associated with certain events. A clearing might become known for a great hunt, a stream for a terrible accident and a tree for the fire from the sky in a great storm. Some places might have become linked with happy events and others feared as places to avoid. These places might even have taken on some responsibility for the events that occurred there, and that some things happened because of the place where it happened!

These initial superstitions must have been the first stirrings of religion, which would come to influence the lives of the people of this land for thousands of years to come.

Slowly over time, the landscape became more than just a source of food. It became a home, a place to live, a place to be responsible for, a place to respect and a place to worship.

It is possible that certain natural features came to have greater significance than others. The mountain out of which the Sun rose or set, the spring where endless pure water bubbled out of the ground or the great rock on the hillside. Even old trees which, to the people of the time would have seemed almost as permanent as the rocks and streams, became places where people met and ceremonies took place.

What is certain is that even thousands of years later monuments were still being built beside these natural features, showing that their importance remained in the social memory and that a feeling of respect continued for these very special places.

It is not clear quite how farming first arrived, whether it was brought by new people coming from the south, or that the ideas were simply adopted by the native population. Probably it was a combination of the two, but what is certain is that by about 4,500 BC it had reached southern England and spread to Wales some hundred of years later.

It was most likely a gradual process, adapting an existing way of life that was already managing the surrounding wild plants and animals. Cattle, sheep and pigs began to be domesticated and wheat and beans cultivated in specially cleared areas. Hunting, fishing and gathering would have remained important as a way of supplementing their basic diet. It would have been during the next thousand years that these early Neolithic farmers became settled and farms took the place of territories.

Until this time little would have been built that remains to be seen today, but with the coming of settled communities came the first surviving structures. These were tombs, or longcairns, built to bury the dead. They varied in size and shape from area to area but were all for communal use. Usually a chamber was constructed of huge upright blocks of stone covered with even larger capping stones. This was then buried within a long mound of smaller stones or earth.

The chamber was often entered through a low passage, and the bones of many individuals were placed inside. It is quite likely that the dead were exposed to the elements first as few whole skeletons have been found within them. In some chambers only skulls and thigh bones have been found suggesting that these bones were symbolic and might have been used for ceremonies outside the tomb before being replaced.

This was a society that honoured its dead, and that even after death ancestors were still revered and played a continuing role in the life of those remaining. The dissembling of the bones and the mixing together of the skeletons could well mean that the dead were no longer seen as individuals but had become a part of a communal concept, thought of simply as 'the ancestors'.

Many of these tombs were of a single chamber, with a large capstone supported by four or more upright stones. Good examples of this type are those at Bodowyr on Anglesey and Maen y Bardd in the Carneddau. In the Rhinogs a different design is evident, with very large capstones supported by only a single upright at one end. In the same area, the concept of the burial cairn is taken to its most extravagant form. At Carneddau Hengwm one of the long cairns covers three separate chambers and is over sixty paces long. The main entrance is framed by huge stones creating a fore-court at its widest end while the other trails away to a narrow point. Others such as those at Parc le Breos on the Gower and Capel Garmon in Snowdonia have a complex arrangement of chambers within a longcairn shaped like a human torso.

Contemporary with these early longcairns, were massive enclosures or causewayed camps. These were encircled with banks and ditches with many entrances and could have been used as trading places as well as seasonal settlements and ceremonial centres. Most of these have been found in southern England, but some are known in Scotland, Northern Ireland and Cumbria and it is likely that they also existed in Wales but are now buried beneath later hillforts.

Slightly later came the henges, which were also circular, ceremonial enclosures, again often ringed with a bank and interior ditch. At Bryn Celli

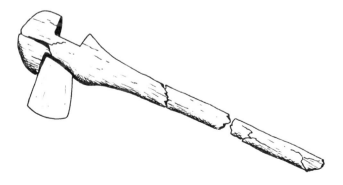

Neolithic stone axe

Ddu on Anglesey, there are the remains of a henge; the bank has all but gone, and the site is now dominated by a later burial chamber built within it. Another one, nearby at Bryn Gwyn, has an outer ditch instead of the more usual inner one. There is some evidence to suggest that these henges had rings of timber posts inside them, possibly with a larger one placed in the centre.

In areas where good hard rock was readily available these timbers circles were often replaced by rings of stones, and it was at this time that the first true stone circles, without the surrounding henge, began to be built. Again, the purpose of these stone circles is a matter of conjecture but it seems that some at least were aligned with the rising and setting of the Sun and the Moon on significant days of the year. It is very likely that religious ceremonies took place within them.

These early henges and circles were large, probably to serve the needs of the large communities of the time. The examples in Wales, however, tend to be much smaller. This could be because the rocky and mountainous nature of much of Wales meant that the land could support far fewer people and smaller communities than the gentle hills of England.

All of these early structures are associated with burial and ceremonial practices. Because of this, it is difficult to discover any details of the day to day lives of these people. From what we do know it can be safely assumed that they lived in a structured and co-operative society. They must have believed in an afterlife or at least a continuity of spirit, resulting in a continuing respect for the dead. They must have had a religion of some sort, and certain places were of religious significance to them.

They had many skills and could make a variety of tools and implements from stone, bone, and wood. Some of these tools, such as stone axes, were developed to such an art form that they became more than just utilitarian. Many examples have been found, beautifully polished, but unused and buried within or close to ceremonial sites.

We also know that they were made from stone found in only a few locations about the country. The axe 'factories' at Cwm Mawr in Mid Wales and Craigllwyd in Snowdonia are examples of such special places; it must be assumed that the place where they were made was of importance and added to the symbolic power of the axe.

As well as stone, they also carved bone, which was shaped into needles and harpoons, and from the few fortunately preserved examples of woodwork, we know they were skilled in this craft too. They could make baskets and fences, and over wet ground they constructed wooden walkways and bridges. They built canoes and rafts, which were capable of crossing not only rivers and lakes but also the open sea. They knew how to make pottery and fire it in simple kilns. They made round-bottomed pots that were both functional and decorative.

We also know that they could quarry because they cut enormous blocks of stone from the hillsides and they also had the technology to transport them over great distances. They could mine, because in eastern England they dug for flint in shafts over 30 feet below ground.

They understood trade and, as farming methods developed, it is likely that a degree of specialism and marketing of produce had begun. They had also started to change the landscape on a significant scale. Great swathes of the forests had by now been cleared to make way for crops and grazing, and the wild woods had retreated into the higher valleys and the steeper slopes of the hills.

If we assume that the Sun and the Moon were important to them, were these their gods? Did they still believe in the 'special places', the mountain-tops, the springs and the caves which their forefathers had so revered? Their circles and burial cairns were so close to these ancient places that it must be assumed that they did, and that although the method of worship developed and changed, the significance of certain special places still held good in the social memory of the people.

Carved idols have been found in stone, wood, and bone, and many of these resemble the enlarged female form. This has led to the belief that

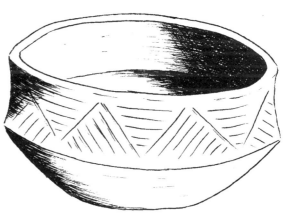

Neolithic pottery

they worshipped an 'earth mother' – an embodiment of the natural forces and features which surrounded them.

Other forms of art are more of a mystery. Geometric patterns of circles and spirals, lozenges and zigzags have been found. More commonly associated with Ireland, this art form can also be seen along the western seaboard of England and Wales. The central stone of Bryn Celli Ddu and the stones of Barclodiad yr Gawres are good examples. What is puzzling is that these carvings were buried within the tombs. If they were not meant to be looked at and admired, what was their purpose? Did the carvings convey power to the carver, or to the dead, or did they carry a message that could be taken beyond death. Whatever their purpose, they do show once again that our ancestors were a complex people whose thoughts and beliefs went far beyond simple superstition and were possibly as intricate as those that exist today.

Despite the obvious differences that would have existed in a land of such varied landscapes and climates, everything suggests that this was largely a homogenous and peaceful society. There is little evidence of warfare between tribes and little need for defensive structures, and it has been described as a 'golden age', when man was in harmony with the landscape and with his fellow man. In reality, however, it is more likely that as the Neolithic period drew to a close, the life of the common man in this undoubtedly complex and spiritual society was probably as short and harsh as at any other period of our history.

In all probability, the Bronze Age arrived in Britain largely unnoticed by the majority of its inhabitants. Just another innovation brought by traders or incomers from the south, the ability to use metal. Gold had been known for many years and had been fashioned into ornaments, but it was the discovery of bronze, an alloy of copper and tin, which was the most significant leap forward.

It is quite likely that to the people of the time, other developments had a greater impact on their day to day lives. The weaving of wool to make warm and comfortable clothes and blankets was just one of the many important stepping-stones to civilisation that occurred in this period. The domestication of the horse would have begun to revolutionise travel, especially when combined with the concept of the wheel, the first known examples of which date from about this time. However, it was the coming of the ability to use metal that would kick-start the great social changes that engulfed the country over the next millennia.

Unlike gold, copper could be found quite easily in many areas. In Wales, it outcropped naturally on Anglesey and on the Great Orme near Llandudno, a major complex of shafts and passages is known to date from this time. Once it was discovered that it could be mixed with tin to make a metal harder than either of them, a new industry and a new era dawned.

On a practical level, it would have made little difference, although it became possible to make very sharp and durable blades and tools, but probably of more significance was the mystique that would have surrounded the process. If the 'magic' which created the shiny metal was strong, so too was the 'magic' which the blades themselves possessed.

Just as some stone axes were symbolically potent, even more so would

Carved stone from Bryn Celli Ddu

be these new objects of bronze. Their importance can be gauged by the number of them found buried with the dead or within circles and barrows.

In the same way, the people who possessed such powerful symbols would have held a status unthought of before. Despite the widespread occurrence of copper, tin could only be found in Cornwall and so bronze would have remained a rare and much-valued material. This rarity combined with the skill required to forge tools from it would have greatly added to the 'power' of possessing them.

The homogenous society of the early Neolithic had already begun to break up, but there came a sudden rise in the number of people who seemed to have held a higher status in society than the common man. The era of the large communal burial site came to an end and, from then on, it seems that only certain individuals were buried within large and imposing cairns and tumuli.

Individual stone coffins, or cists, held a single body, often accompanied by grave goods indicative of their wealth. Bronze axes and arrowheads, jewellery and ornaments were placed alongside the bodies, and with them were ceremonial beakers containing food and water to accompany the soul to the afterlife. There is even some evidence to suggest that flowers were placed on the bodies, in a custom that continues to the present day. In other areas, bodies were cremated and the ashes placed within a pot before a final burial. These cremation pots were often inserted into existing cairns and tumuli.

These people have become known as the Beaker People, and it was long supposed that they were an influx or 'invasion' of people from the continent, who revolutionised the way of life in Britain. More likely, was that it was the ideas which spread, possibly by new settlers, to the indigenous population who then adopted them.

The tumuli which covered all these high status burials were no longer the longcairns of old, but round barrows, thousands of which still lie scattered across our countryside. They are found in a variety of forms and sizes, some built of earth and others of stone. Some were ringed with a ditch and bank while others consisted simply of a circle of small stones surrounding an open space.

Near Llyn Brenig is a fine restored example of just such a ringcairn and it is believed that a large wooden pole once stood at its centre. Later the open central space was filled in to create yet another variation known as a platform cairn.

In some of them, the cairn material was held in place by a ring of large stones around the base. These are called kerbed cairns, and in some instances the kerb has remained long after the cairn itself has been worn away or destroyed.

Just as the barrows were changing size and shape, so too did the stone circles. The few circles that were built in the Neolithic period had been large and widely spaced across the country. With the coming of the Bronze Age their numbers increased tremendously and their size diminished. Most of the circles of Wales date from this period and are relative small.

In some places, several circles were built close together. Perhaps each served a different family group, or it could be that over time new circles simply replaced the older ones. Some were true circles and others elliptical, and some even had a large central stone. Some were built on artificially levelled platforms and some were graduated with the tallest stones placed opposite the smallest. Some were tiny and barely circles at all, consisting of only four or five small stones. The Four Stones near Radnor is a good example in Wales, although this type is more commonly associated with Scotland and Ireland.

Most individual standing stones also date from this era. Again, their purpose is difficult to interpret. Many stand close to cir-

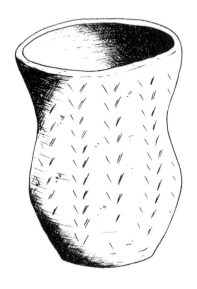

Bronze Age beaker

cles as outliers and may have been used to mark the rising or setting of the Sun on significant days.

Others definitely marked the routes of the many ancient trackways that crossed the land. Along the track that runs just inland from the west coast of Wales between Towyn and Porthmadoc, many of the ancient stones still line the route. In the northern Carneddau, the great stone of Maen Penddu stands at an important crossroads where two major routeways met. In other places, the stones surround an important site. On Anglesey, the standing stones near Llanfairynghornwy form a partial ring around a small rocky hillock known as Pen yr Orsedd, 'the hill of the throne', a place of significance. At nearby Llanfechell the stones themselves are the focus of the site where three tall stones crown a high hill.

There are also examples of rows of stones close together and running away from, or towards, circles and cairns. A small stone row can still be seen near the famous waterfall of Pistyll Rhaeadr in Mid Wales.

As the Bronze Age ended, the break-up of society into regional tribal groupings became more intense. Individuals of high status rose to power and rivalries between areas and tribes developed. This was fuelled by the problems of a rising population and an increasing competition for land.

The era of megalithic monuments began to wane and the custom of circle building slowly died out, although there is some evidence to suggest that they continued to be used and remained as sacred places for a long time to come. It was at about this time, about 1,000 BC that there was also a general deterioration in the weather. It became much colder and wetter and the upland areas became no longer viable for farming. This would have added to the growing pressure on the already crowded and deforested lowlands. The result of this would have been the need for communities to defend or take land to sustain themselves, resulting for the first time in the construction of defensive sites and the significant production of weapons for more than just hunting.

This rise in aggression between tribal groups would have been made worse by yet another innovation which reached Britain by about 800 BC, the smelting of iron!

Easy to find and to extract, iron was very different from bronze. The 'power' of these new weapons came not just from the symbolic importance of their possession, but in their use. Powerful weapons lead to the rise of powerful individuals and groups. Warlords rose by strength and tribal boundaries were made and broken as the fortunes of war ebbed and flowed. Great forts were built on the hills, defended by huge banks and ditches. Their still-substantial remains are still widely scattered across the hilltops of Wales.

Bronze Age hut

For most people burials were largely unmarked, although in eastern England at least, the great chieftains were entombed with their war chariots beneath large circular tumuli. Perhaps as life became more violent, death became less significant, and perhaps even the power of the old gods lessened as the power of iron weapons increased.

What we do know is that the stone circles and henges were gradually abandoned and, although they were still seen as special places, the people seem to have returned to their older beliefs. Again, it was the natural features of the landscape, the pools and springs, trees and caves that became the focus of their religion. A priesthood grew up and these 'Druids' surrounded themselves in a lore which to the common man must have seemed both magical and mystical.

These changes happened slowly as society continued to evolve and develop largely from within although trade across the Channel and the Irish Sea ensured a gradual flow and exchange of ideas and innovations. So it would have continued, had it not been for the most cataclysmic event ever to occur in our long history. On one fateful day in the spring of 43 BC, the first of the vast legions of Rome set foot in Britain. With them they brought a culture which would sweep through England and Wales and supersede if not completely replace all that had existed before. They also

Iron Age roundhouse

brought with them the written word and so ended for ever the prehistory of our land.

So what, if anything, have our prehistoric ancestors left us? Is there anything beyond the few abandoned stones and mounds that lie scattered across our hills? The answer is yes, they have left us much more. In fact, their legacy is the very foundation stone on which our modern civilisation is built.

The people of Wales, at least in part, still speak a language that has its roots in prehistory. Many words still in use today might well have been recognisable to the people who raised the great stones thousands of years ago.

Many of the older churchyards of Wales are still circular in shape, built within and upon ancient stone circles, while others stand beside natural springs and ancient wells. The continuity of these special sites remains and many of us still worship in the same places as did our distant ancestors.

Many of the religious ceremonies which the Christian faith still celebrate throughout the year were 'borrowed' from the older faiths, and we still decorate Yule Logs, paint Easter eggs and kiss beneath the mistletoe. We continue, often unknowingly, traditions more ancient than we imagine.

Many of these old beliefs and customs still cling on, often as no more than superstitions, but every time we 'touch wood' or toss a coin into a pool we are reaching back into the past, touching a time and a place that we do not realise that we remember.

The ancient stones are a part of us and we a part of them. We owe it to our children, and to our children's children to care for them and preserve them. We must respect them as a part of our heritage, a part of what makes us what we are, and remember that they are our window back into the time before History began.

South Wales

Trefach standing stone beneath the Mynydd Carningli

1. Pentre Ifan
Newport

Approx. distance: 7 miles

Approx. time: 4 hours

Starting point: Cilgwyn, GR 075367

Grade: A magnificent, well-marked walk over rolling hills

O.S. Outdoor Leisure sheet: 35

Grid references: Pentre Ifan burial chamber, GR 100370; standing stones, GR 091357; Banc Du stones, GR 077346; Gellifawr standing stone, GR 064351

Just inland from the Pembrokeshire coast at Newport, rises Mynydd Carningli, 'the peak of the angels'. Its rocky tors still dominate the surrounding landscape as they would have done over five thousand years ago when the great stones of Pentre Ifan were first raised. This famous burial chamber sits in glorious isolation on a gentle slope facing out to sea within clear view of its jagged summit ridge.

This whole landscape is a treasure, largely ignored by the many visitors who flock to the nearby coast without realising the delights which lie just a few miles inland. High and wild hills, crowned with jagged rocks, tower over lonely valleys and ancient woodlands. Prehistoric trackways, still often marked with standing stones, snake across the hills and open heathland.

This circular walk has it all, prehistoric sites and primordial forests, high hills and rocky crags. It follows quiet lanes winding through the valleys and forgotten tracks over the lonely moors, and to cap it all, it visits the most spectacular of the Neolithic sites in the whole of Wales.

It begins in Cilgwyn, a scattered hamlet on either side of an old bridge over a tributary of the Afon Gwaun. From the bridge, a tiny lane runs eastwards to a junction where a left turn takes you to an isolated chapel which faces directly towards the hills behind. The route continues past the chapel to a lane leading to Fachongle Ganol. At its end is a footpath, which takes you towards the ancient woodland of Tycanol. An open area of scattered trees and gorse is entered before the woodland proper is reached, and here the route is not immediately obvious. Look about, and partially hidden beneath the dark canopy of the ancient trees is a stile, which allows you to enter.

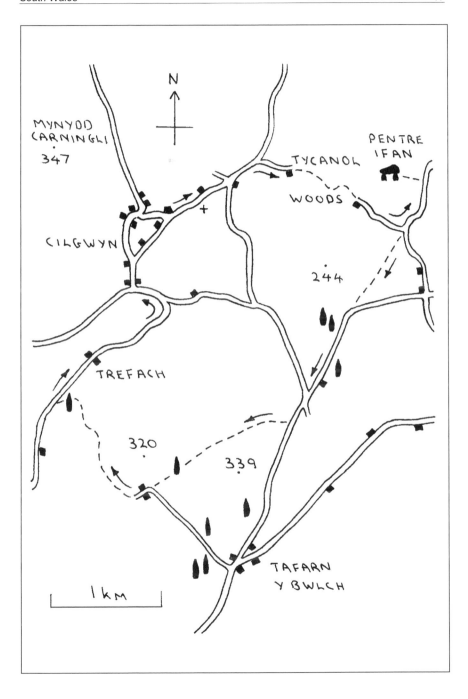

This is a breathtaking place of trees and rocks festooned with moss and lichen, and tiny ferns grow in the crooks of the branches. When I last passed through it, I saw woodpeckers and nuthatches and a large dog fox, which wandered, oblivious to my presence, along the path in front. Many of the trees are twisted and gnarled and hang over the path as if straight from a page of Tolkien. One could easily imagine Tom Bombadil striding purposefully between their mossy trunks. The wood is still managed, with coppicing and selective grazing being used just as it would have been in times past to preserve its unique flora and fauna. The whole area, which includes open heathland and rough pasture, is known as Tycanol Woods, but the heart of the forest where the oldest trees survive still keeps the wonderful name of Hagr y coed, 'the wild wood'. If time allows, turn off the main path and wander a while in the dappled shadows of its ancient canopy.

Our route crosses only a small corner of this last remnant of a much greater forest which once blanketed all of these high valleys. It takes the main bridleway directly through the wood towards the house of Tycanol. Close to the house is the site of an ancient settlement, which further reinforces the feeling that this extraordinary place has somehow managed to survive the overwhelming changes of the intervening millennia.

Where the path splits, the left fork leads to the house and its driveway can be followed out of the woods to meet a narrow lane at a sharp bend. Turning left, this soon brings you to the footpath for Pentre Ifan.

As soon as you leave the road and turn along the track towards the monument, it leaps into view. The great capstone too high to be true, too streamlined to be ancient and the whole structure too delicate to have survived for over five thousand years. Yet there it is, a huge sixteen-ton capstone perched on just three tall, slender and pointed stones over eight feet above the ground. Other tall stones form an arc at one end, the remains of an entrance forecourt which would have held in place the vast torso-shaped cairn that once covered the burial chamber. Beneath the capstone is an oval, stone-lined pit into which would have been placed the communal remains of the dead. It is now generally believed that ceremonies would have been held within the forecourt, between the truncated legs of the cairn, and that the entrance stones were taken down and replaced regularly.

All trace of the cairn has gone, almost certainly the result of a deliberate exposure of the internal stones at a later period of its history, but several other large stones still lie scattered around the site. What remains is a delight, architecturally magnificent and sited in wonderful isolation looking out to sea and beneath the jagged tors of the Carningli. It is a place to sit

The mysterious Tycanol Woods

and imagine, to soak up the atmosphere that pervades the ancient site. The
stones themselves are of beautiful blue dolerite, like the bluestones of
Stonehenge, rough to the touch but smooth and shapely to the eye.

Surely this could never have been a simple, utilitarian place of burial. It
must have been a statement of great respect for those that it held, or the
place to which their spirits were departing. This is no rough 'caveman'
structure but a sleek and sophisticated symbol of a society that must have
possessed values beyond our present knowledge or understanding.

After returning to the road and following it back to the lane for Tycanol,
the obvious bridleway is taken which leads straight up the hillside ahead.
The path is deeply entrenched between high banks of gorse and ferns and
purple heather, until it opens out near the top of the slope. This is Carnedd
Meibion-Owen, and it is crowned with four separate rocky tors. These
steep outcrops of blue dolerite rise above the rounded hilltop and it would
have been from jumbled rock piles such as these that the stones for Pentre
Ifan and even Stonehenge would have been taken. They afford a magnificent view in all directions. To the south, the long ridge of the Mynydd
Preseli, to the west Mynydd Carningli and away to the north the sparkling
water of Cardigan Bay. Nearer at hand, Pentre Ifan is just visible amongst

Pentre Ifan

the fields below and even closer are two small standing stones beside the lane that climbs over the shoulder of the hill.

This lane is followed past the paired stones and another single one in the field to the left, to where it begins to climb again towards the higher hills ahead. A not very obvious paths turn off to the right and soon becomes a good track climbing up and around the shoulder of Waun Mawr to a high col between its top and the next hill. This route is lined with small standing stones and on the high point of the pass is a strange but obviously ancient site. One large stone leans but still stands beside three smaller ones and one which has fallen, amidst scattered cairn material, but too little remains to say what this might originally have looked like.

Beyond this high point the path drops to a remote farm and passes through it to where a rough track leads out to the west. This peters out into a well-marked path, which crosses high fields littered with large blocks of stone and seems to head directly for the summit of Mynydd Carningli away beyond the upper Gwaun Valley. This is high open sheep country and the walking is easy and the views superb. Buzzards circle above, spiralling up on the rising air, their eerie cries carrying on the wind.

The track is still marked with the occasional upright stone and, before long, a tall standing stone appears directly ahead. This pointed, eight-foot bluestone stands beside the track which, at this point, lines up with the summit ridge of Mynydd Carningli beyond. The path then curls around the stone and heads for a gate leading onto the road.

The way back to Cilgwyn is straightforward, following the lane pleasantly down, across the hillside, admiring the gradually changing scene away to the left. At the bottom of the hill, a left and right turn brings you back into the village.

On the occasions that I have done this walk I have seen few people and even fewer cars. The most common form of transport seems to be horses and the almost accepted background drone of traffic is blissfully absent. Even the few visitors, who manage to negotiate the tangled web of narrow lanes to reach Pentre Ifan itself, whisper quietly in its hallowed presence. And in Tycanol Woods, nothing disturbs the sound of the birds but the wind in the leaves. It is a rare privilege to sit beneath its gnarled boughs and experience its hushed and ancient stillness.

2. Gors Fawr
Mynydd Preseli

Approx. distance: 7 miles

Approx. time: 4 hours

Starting point: Mynachlog-ddu, GR 144306

Grade: Easy walk along quiet lanes and over open heathland

O.S. Outdoor Leisure sheet: 35

Grid references: Gors Fawr stone circle, GR 134294; Gors Fawr standing stones, GR 135295; Cwm Gawr standing stones, GR 118310; Rhos Fach standing stones, GR 135305; Waun Lwyd standing stones, GR 157313

On the southern slopes of the Mynydd Preseli is a wild landscape of open heath and marsh known as the Gors Fawr, 'the great bog'. Even today, partly reclaimed by farmland and crossed by moorland roads, it still possesses a unique and timeless atmosphere. Drained by the headwaters of the Eastern or Black Cleddau, the Gors Fawr is a wilderness of stone, reeds and gorse. On its higher margins sheep graze on the rich turf between the rocks, and thickets of hawthorn and alder straggle along beside the twisting streams.

Preserved within the moor are a fascinating legacy of paired standing stones and the only surviving stone circle in this corner of Wales. The pairs of stones are a real mystery, their purpose or meaning lost long ago when they were abandoned to the sheep and the wild ponies. Each of the pairs of stones stands on rising ground around the edge of the moor, and each pair are about three paces apart. None of them seems to align with anything in particular or to face in any significant direction. Were they doorways or portals into 'the great bog', where, hidden away deep within its inner fastness, was the circle? Were they entrances to settlements or camps that were lived in by the people who worshiped on the moor?

To visit these ancient places, our walk begins in Mynachlog-ddu, a small and sleepy village up on the edge of the heath, sitting between two of the streams which run down from the high spine of the mountains. The route takes the tiny lane heading south, which crosses over a bridge and climbs up onto the lower slopes of the hills. At first, the lane runs between overhanging trees, but soon it opens out giving views across towards Foel Cwmberwyn, the highest of the Mynydd Preseli.

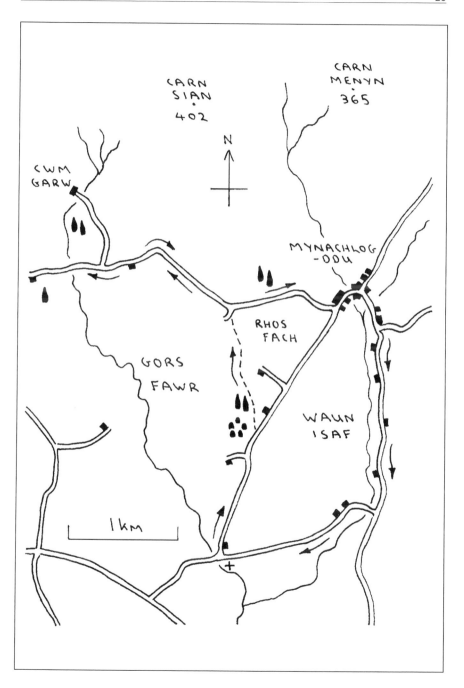

Down below is the Waun Isaf, 'the lower moor', a wild and uncultivated arm of the Gors Fawr. The lane climbs higher, and on the steep bank falling away to the right is a last remnant of the ancient woodland that must once have cloaked the lower slopes of the hills. A right turn is taken and the lane crosses the river again, rises over the shoulder of the hill and drops once more to where the little church of St Dogmael stands above another tributary of the Cleddau. This ancient church is built within an even older circular enclosure. In the 12th century it was a chapel belonging to the Benedictine Abbey of St Dogmael near Cardigan, and is almost certainly responsible for the naming of Mynachlog-ddu as 'the place of the black monks'.

At the junction our route turns right and climbs up the long hill between high hedges topped with ash trees. At the top, the long undulating spine of the Mynydd Preseli appears ahead with the rocky tors of Carnmenyn drawing the eye. The lane is now running along a ridge of slightly higher ground, which might once have been a small island of drier land within the marsh. On this rise, off to the left of the lane, is the circle of Gors Fawr.

Sixteen tiny stones stand in a ring amongst the scattered gorse bushes and natural rocks. None of them stands more than about three feet high and they decrease in height from the south to the north. Several of the stones have fallen but are still in place and none appear to be missing. There are some stones lying in the grass within the ring but whether they are natural rocks or the remains of a central structure is not clear.

It is a marvellous place to sit and soak up the atmosphere of the heath. Around the circle the sheep graze on the short-cropped grass, but not far beyond it the moor sweeps away into reedbeds, and thickets of tangled undergrowth mark the lines of the streams weaving their way south to join the Cleddau. Several footpaths are marked on the map crossing the Gors Fawr but all seem to peter out in the primeval wilderness at its centre.

About a hundred metres off to the north-east stand two outlying stones, both almost six feet tall, at least double the height of the stones in the circle. They are about sixteen paces apart and differ from the other paired stones of the moor, which are all much closer together. It has been suggested that these two giant bluestones line up with a dip on the horizon where the sun rises on midsummer morning, a date of great significance, and as such, marked with ceremonies of some kind within the circle. It is fascinating to imagine what might have taken place there, surrounded by the stones, which were themselves surrounded by the all but impenetrable marshland. Who would have stood there, within that inner sanctum as the Sun rose over the hills away to the north-east?

The walk continues past the outliers, past the white cottage and follows

Gors Fawr stone circle

a narrow strip of short turf towards a group of scattered buildings and sheep pens ahead. It carries on past the rather incongruous skeleton of an old bus, which now acts as a shelter from the sun and the rain for the sheep. The path then becomes a farm track leading to a narrow moorland road crossing the heath.

This can be followed easily back to Mynachlog-ddu to shorten the walk, but it is pleasant to turn the other way and head westwards, climbing up onto the lower slopes of Carn Sian. This gain of height allows you to look out over the moor to the low hills of Carmarthenshire.

This is a wonderful area of yellow gorse and high reeds, and birds are everywhere. Stonechats balance on the gorse and 'click' constantly like two stones being tapped together. Curlews call and, up in the sky, buzzards cry mournfully as they spiral up on the rising air.

As the lane rounds the shoulder of Carn Sian, it begins to drop gradually down into Cwm Garw, 'the rough valley'. Away to the right beside the stream is the first of the paired standing stones. A pointed stone about eight feet tall stands about four paces from a slightly shorter and very thin, leaning pillar. Although they can be seen quite clearly from the road, it is possible to reach them across the open moor by weaving between the gorse bushes beside the stream.

From this point our route returns to where we first joined the lane and continues over the Rhos Fach, 'the small moor'. Almost immediately two large standing stones appear, one on either side of the lane. Unfortunately, neither is genuine! The one on the right is a memorial to someone called 'Waldo', while the one on the left was one of two local bluestones raised in recent times, here and at Stonehenge, to mark the link between the two areas. It was stones from the Mynedd Preseli that were used to create the first circle at that famous site. How they were carried all that way, is a mystery which still has not been satisfactorily answered.

However, two genuine stones are less than a hundred metres away, hidden behind gorse bushes in the field to the left. This second pair is very similar to the one in Cwm Garw, although the stones are not quite as tall. Again, a large heavy stone stands beside a shorter slender one. If not portals, is it possible that they represented the male and female forms, and were intended as a symbol of fertility? Another pair can be found just beyond Mynachlog-ddu on the Waun Lwyd, or 'grey moor', and another to the south, near Glandy Cross. We will probably never know the true answer!

It is interesting that passers-by stop to look at the recently erected stones and it is a popular picnic area, yet less than a hundred metres away are two ancient and mysterious stones that sit almost unnoticed and forgotten. Perhaps it is the moor itself that holds the magic, and the stones both ancient and modern simply stand as symbols of our reverence.

While pondering such deep and weighty matters, it is but a short walk down, off the moor and back to Mynachlog-ddu.

The paired stones of Rhos Fach

3. Carreg Samson
St David's

Approx. distance: 4 miles

Approx. time: 3 hours

Starting point: Trefin, GR 840325

Grade: A short but spectacular walk along exposed cliff-top paths

O.S. Outdoor Leisure sheet: 35

Grid references: Castell Coch Iron Age fort, GR 840338; Carreg Sampson burial chamber, GR 848335; Mathry burial chamber, GR 868317

The St David's peninsula juts out into the Irish Sea at the extreme south-west tip of Wales. On its spectacular north coast, high up above the waves, lie the ruins of a once great burial chamber. Like so many others of the ancient Welsh monuments, they seem to have more in common with those of Ireland than with those beyond the mountains in England. This one stands in a high field and looks out towards that distant and unseen land.

Our walk begins in Trefin, a pretty village perched up on a low rocky hillock above the coast. It takes the quiet lane out to the west in the direction of the neighbouring village of Llanrhian, leaving the last cottages behind, dropping down towards the sea and the cove of Aber Draw. On the grassy slopes just beyond is a dramatic-looking, but only recently erected stone circle. At the bottom of the hill, beside the remains of an old watermill, a good path leads off to the right crossing over a small bridge and climbing up steeply above the rocky cliffs.

Within moments this leads you up into a visual wonderland. Away to the west the cliffs rise towards the rocky promontory of Trwyn Elen, 'the headland of the deer', and in front of it the dramatic island of Ynys-fach. Beyond them in the far distance, the shapely peaks of Penberry and Carn Llidi tower up above the rugged coast. On my last visit in August, wild flowers splashed vivid colours over the steep slopes above the rocks. Purple heather and yellow gorse shone bright between the deep green of the ferns and clumps of thistle-like knapweed, foxgloves and delicate yellow vetch grew in tangled confusion beside the path. To the north a vast seascape stretched away to banks of cloud low on the horizon.

At the top of the first headland, the view widens even further, with

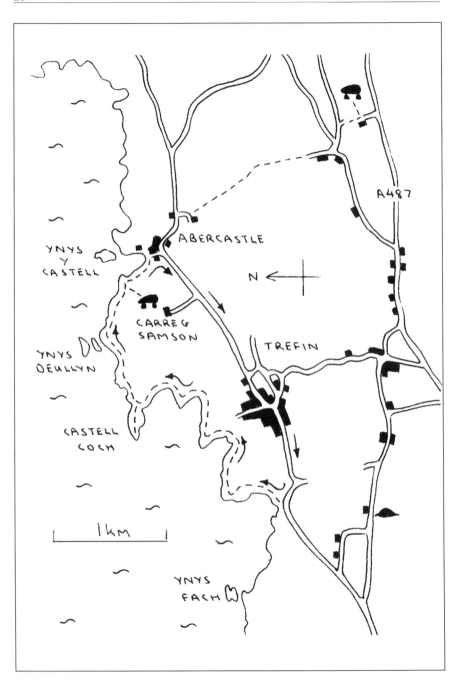

Carreg Samson

headland after headland jutting out into the sea, slowly fading away to the north-east. Beyond them all is Strumble Head, and its dominant hilltop of Garn Fawr, 'the great rock', hazy in the distance.

The path is wonderful, rising and falling with the cliff top, at times running across the adjacent fields and at others perched precariously on the very edge of the cliffs. Below, the rocks fall in jagged ridges into the sea, where natural caves and arches have been carved by the ceaseless action of the waves. At the end of each headland, stacks and small islands stand as brief testimony to the destruction caused by the tremendous power of the sea. Above it all, gulls wheel and cry, stiff-winged fulmars glide in and out of the steep-sided coves and ravens tumble and dive over the cliffs.

The path skirts around three rocky coves, each unreachable except by boat, to arrive at the long headland of Castell Coch, 'the red castle'. This was a fortified encampment in Iron Age times, and a more impregnable site is difficult to imagine. On all sides, except where a narrow natural causeway links it to the mainland, this promontory is surrounded by precipitous cliffs which fall to jagged rocks and crashing waves. The only entrance is guarded by two high stone banks and a deep rock-cut ditch, which runs from cliff edge to cliff edge.

Collapsed burial chamber near Mathry

Beyond the defences is a beautiful area of mostly level grassland which, despite being exposed to the westerly wind, must have been a marvellous place to live or at least to retreat to when danger threatened. It is well worth walking out to the very end to where it rises slightly and narrows before everything ends in a sudden and dramatic plunge into the swirling waters below. A single free-standing stack stands sentry-like off the end of the headland as if guarding the settlement above.

Beyond the fort, the rugged coastline continues towards the island of Ynys Deullyn. I watched seals below the island being pestered by a group of great black-backed gulls that swooped and dived at them before returning each time to an isolated rock beneath the cliffs. From the islands, the path drops gradually down towards the narrow inlet of Abercastle.

Just before it reaches it, a path branches off to the right, climbing up to fields beside a large farm. In the first field stands Carreg Samson, 'Samson's stone'. Now only the main burial chamber remains although other large stones, which must once have formed part of the great chambered cairn, still lie about the field margins. The stones of the covering cairn have long gone, probably incorporated into the nearby wall.

The capstone is huge, over five paces long and of enormous weight, yet it has remained supported on only three relatively flimsy uprights for all these thousands of years. Three other uprights still stand, although they play no part in holding the weight of the great stone roof. The capstone and three of the uprights are of a rough composite rock and each has large veins and star-shaped splashes of orangey quartz running through them. The other three are much darker and smoother in texture. Within the tomb is an oval chamber, over four paces long and high enough to stand up in.

Local legend has it that the capstone was put into place by St Samson who raised it by using just one finger. On the nearby island of Ynys Deullyn is an ancient mound which, in keeping with the legend, is also known as 'the grave of Samson's finger'.

From the stones, the route returns to the coastal path, which drops quickly down steps into the perfect natural harbour of Abercastle. On the far side of the narrow cove is another islet known as Ynys y Castell, 'castle island', which must also have been a fortified site in the past. The little village is very picturesque, with pastel-coloured cottages looking down onto a small harbour and slipway full of boats of all descriptions. The coastal path continues on along the coast for many more miles and it is with great reluctance that we leave it and turn inland in order to return to Trefin.

About two miles away to the south-east is another burial chamber hidden away amongst the fields and hedges near to Mathry. It is largely ruined and partly buried within a large overgrown bank. The huge capstone is still obvious, although only two collapsed uprights can still be seen beneath it and several other large stones have been built into the bank. In the field next to it is a small standing stone which was possibly connected to it, or marked a trackway leading to it.

This can be reached by taking bridleways and footpaths from Abercastle but it is an unspectacular site and very difficult to locate. For those who like an adventure, try to find it, not many do!

Much better to return to Trefin along the narrow but quiet lane which climbs up out of Abercastle. Deep-cut between high banks and overhung with trees initially, it soon levels out and gives the occasional fleeting views out to the north and back towards Strumble Head. Within no time at all you will have arrived back in Trefin.

This is a short walk, but one which allows you to visit a dramatic ancient site set amid scenery which is both spectacular and little changed from when it was built over five thousand years ago. On a calm day the waves lap gently around the rocks and the air is alive with butterflies and bees, the sky stretching in a vast arc from horizon to horizon. But when the weather turns, it can be a fearsome place. The westerly winds drive huge waves to pound against the cliffs and the air is filled with noise and spray. Whatever the mood of the sea, Carreg Samson still seems to turn its back to the land and face outwards, over the water towards distant Garn Fawr and perhaps even further, away across the sea towards its spiritual homeland in Ireland.

4. Cefn Bryn
The Gower

Approx. distance: 10 miles

Approx. time: 5 hours

Starting point: Llanrhidian, GR 497923

Grade: A long and strenuous walk over open heathland and fields, with one short section along a busy road

O.S. Explorer sheet: 164

Grid references: Cilifor Top Iron Age fort, GR 507924; tumulus, GR 511914; Maen Cetty burial chamber, GR 492906; cairn, GR 490905; Samson's Jack, GR 477922

The Gower Peninsula juts out into the Bristol Channel from the heart of industrial South Wales. Running along its centre like a spine is a great hill known as Cefn Bryn, 'the ridge'. In ancient times, this long whaleback would have been an important trackway connecting together the many settlements that were then scattered along its flanks. At its eastern end it rises from the sea at Oxwich Bay, and in the west is linked by a further ridge of high ground to Llanmadoc Hill and Rhossili Down. Evidence of the ancient civilisation that once thrived here can still be found all along this range of beautiful hills. Our walk follows just a short section of the ancient trackway.

It begins in Llanrhidian, a sizeable village to the north of Cefn Bryn, which straddles the slope between the wide coastal marshes and the central heathland. For just a short distance the route follows the main road eastwards towards Swansea until a tiny lane branches off to the left towards the Welsh Moor. This climbs up to where a concessionary footpath leads up to Cilifor Top, which is crowned by an Iron Age fort. The small hilltop has a double bank and ditch on the southern and western sides and is defended by steep natural slopes on the others. It gives a wonderful view away to the south and west and is an ideal spot to plan the walk ahead.

After returning to the lane, the walk continues along it until a track turns off to the right. This enters and then follows a narrow strip of old oak woodland to a muddy lane running back to the main road. This is crossed to reach the unfenced moorland road that rises up and over the high ridge of Cefn Bryn. This can be followed easily, but much pleasanter is to branch

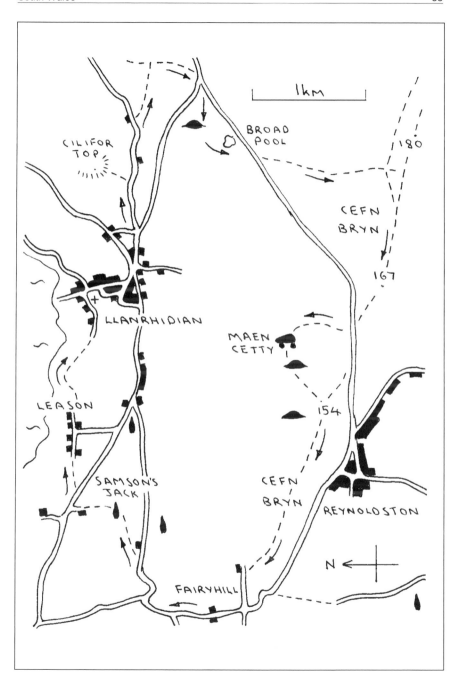

off to the right across the open heath. Head initially towards a large fern covered mound, which is in fact a Bronze Age burial mound, before circling back to rejoin the road just beyond the still waters of the Broad Pool.

About 150 metres past the pool, a faint but reasonably obvious path leads off to the left towards the high ridge. It heads directly for the obvious corner of a strip of woodland running across the slope.

Within seconds, the road is out of sight, and you are on the open heath – empty, beautiful, and quiet. Wild ponies and sheep have cropped the turf and dwarf heather and gorse add swathes of colour across the undulating landscape. Tiny yellow tormentil flowers shine like stars in the short grass and clumps of taller ferns and reeds add deeper shades of green to the patchwork moorland. Skylarks hang in the sky and tiny pipits flit between the scattered rocks.

As the path reaches the corner of the woodland, it crosses a small stream and then steepens and climbs up towards the ridge. It soon joins a good track, which can be followed to the right to reach the skyline.

Once there you find yourself on the very backbone of the Peninsula, with sweeping views in all directions. To the west, a multi-coloured collage of fields and woodland stretches away towards Rhossili Down, and to the south Oxwich Bay shines between its high headlands.

This is the line of the ancient trackway and it is easily followed westwards along the crest of the ridge. On a slight rise is a viewfinder, which points out the distant outlines of the Mynydd Preseli and the Brecon Beacons, with Lundy Island just visible away to the south. Beyond the viewing point, the path drops down to meet the road as it crosses a dip in the ridge.

Beyond it and just visible is the Maen Cetty, otherwise known, like so many others in Wales, as Arthur's Stone. It is easily approached along a pleasant grass swath, and from a distance it looks just like an enormous natural boulder lying on the hillside. As you reach it, its true identity as a purposely constructed burial chamber becomes almost unbelievably obvious. But how on Earth did ancient man manage to manoeuvre such a colossal rock into position? It defies belief, as even with the knowledge of modern technology the task would appear truly daunting! It is not so much its length or its width but its solidity. Being taller than it is wide its weight must be immense.

To add to the unworldliness of its appearance is the fact that it is perched rather precariously on just a few tiny, and seemingly unsubstantial uprights! In fact, of the nine that remain, only two seem to take its entire weight, with a third helping to keep it in balance. How it has remained in place for so long is amazing!

The cairn sits in a hollow, surrounded by many smaller stones and sev-

Maen Cetty

eral larger ones, which may originally have been part of an entrance passage. The original cairn appears to have been roughly circular and about twenty-four paces across. It is usually assumed that the smaller cairn stones were taken to build nearby field walls, but this cannot be the case with Maen Cetty as the nearest wall is probably a mile away. This puzzle of the missing stones could well be answered by a large Bronze Age cairn, which is only a hundred metres away and still virtually intact. Perhaps one was robbed to build the other? If this seems irreverent, it must be remembered that over a thousand years may have separated the building of the two sites. It has also been suggested that the ancient dolmens, or 'stone tables', were intentionally exposed as part of a later religious cult.

From the burial chamber, it is possible to take a path which passes the cairn and circles back towards the trig point, and is clearly obvious on the crest of the ridge. Another cairn lies away to the right and can also be visited. From the high point, a pleasant track follows the high ground as it gently drops down, passing several large rocks of wonderful white and rose quartz, to meet a farm track leading to a narrow lane.

In the past, this area was littered with standing stones, many in groups and alignments, but unfortunately not many remain and even fewer can be visited. One of the few that has survived is Samson's Jack, probably because of its immense size. To reach it, our route takes the lane past the Fairyhill Hotel to where it joins the rather busier road. Care should be taken as this has no pavement. It is followed up the hill and around sharp bends to where a signposted path leads away to the left through a farmyard.

In the fields beyond, and partly hidden behind the large hedge to the left of the path, is the great stone. It is at least twelve feet high and made of white quartz. With many of the other nearby stones removed, it is difficult to work out whether it once formed part of an alignment of stones or marked a route. However, it is noticeable that as you approach the stone, Maen Cetty is clearly visible, exactly on the skyline of Cefn Bryn away to the south-east.

The path rejoins a lane for a short distance, with Weobley Castle just beyond, until another path turns off across fields to the left. This is well

Samson's Jack

signposted; it crosses several small fields and leads to the small and pretty hamlet of Leason. It then drops down a steep, but rather overgrown bank to a good track leading back into Llanrhidian. It re-enters the village beside the old church, where it crosses a stream over a lovely old stone-slabbed bridge.

On the sloping green outside the church are two large standing stones, one at least of which appears to be a genuinely ancient stone.

This is a long and very varied walk, but one which is well worth the effort. On the section along the trackway of Cefn Bryn, it is very easy to imagine the landscape and the ancient sites as they once were. Down in the valleys more has changed and the seemingly indiscriminate scattering of standing stones ask more questions than they answer. But then, what else would you expect on the still wild and mysterious Gower Peninsula!

5. Tinkinswood
Vale of Glamorgan

Approx. distance: 5 miles

Approx. time: 3 hours 30 mins

Starting point: St Nicholas, GR 091743

Grade: A well-marked walk over fields and along quiet lanes

O.S. Explorer sheet: 151

Grid references: Tinkinswood burial chamber, GR 093733; St Lythans burial chamber, GR 101723; site of tumulus, GR 106741; ancient quarry site, GR 094733

In the gentle hills of the Vale of Glamorgan lies one of the oldest and most evocative megalithic monuments of Wales. The great Neolithic chambered cairn of Tinkinswood was built as long ago as 4,000 BC and remains one of the most amazing feats of prehistoric construction to be found anywhere in the World.

To reach it, our walk begins in St Nicholas, a small village which lies barely three miles from the outskirts of Cardiff. Despite this, the country-side around is quiet and pretty, and only a line of pylons striding across the hills reminds you of the great city not far away. From the old church with its even older yew trees, you cross the main road and turn down a quiet lane towards the well-known Dyffryn Gardens. After about three hundred metres, a footpath turns off to the right and leads gently down through rolling sheep fields, past stands of tall mature trees until, partially hidden in a wood, the great capstone of Tinkinswood comes into view. As you approach it, it grows in size until you stand beside the largest megalithic stone ever raised in Britain. Nearly ten paces long and half as wide, it has been estimated to weigh almost fifty tons and covers a large, stone lined, single chamber.

It is of a type known as the Severn-Cotswold monuments, which date back to the early Neolithic period. It was originally covered with a long mound in the shape of a stylised female torso, the outline of which is still clearly visible. The capstone slopes backwards, the front supported by three large stones, between which a low circular gap allowed access to the chamber. Only one of the huge side slabs remains, which has opened the

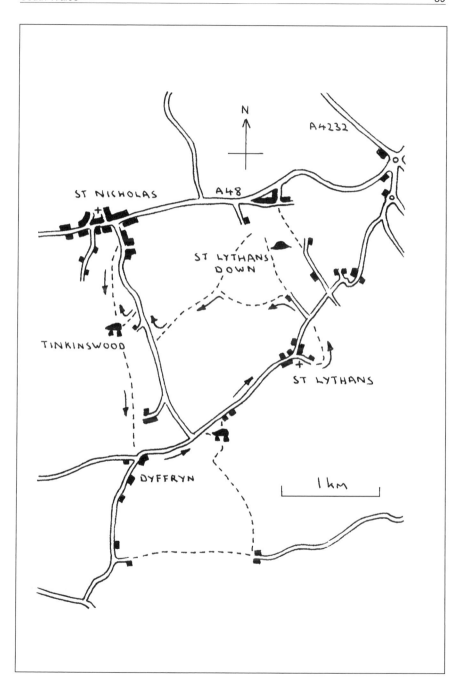

tomb to the elements. The back is supported by a wide but much lower stone.

The rock is a local mudstone, which erodes into fantastic grooves and hollows giving an impression of great fragility that is only belied by its almost unbelievable antiquity. The capstone has, in fact, cracked, and is supported by a brick pillar that was added, rather incongruously, in 1914 when the tomb was excavated.

The entrance, which was placed between the 'legs' of the cairn, was lined with drystone walling built in a herringbone pattern, and has also been restored. This entrance would have been bricked up and only opened occasionally for important ceremonial events. Behind the chamber, the cairn sloped gently downward for fifty paces. An open stone-lined cist is visible to one side of the cairn, and others apparently lie still covered beneath the remaining mound.

Today the longcairn is surrounded on three sides by a dense woodland of hawthorn, beech and ash, which largely obscures a rather intrusive pylon in the next field. It has a pleasant, open aspect to the east and the capstone is a marvellous place to sit and let time pass. I love this place and still find it hard to comprehend that this huge stone was raised well over a thousand years before either the trilithons of Stonehenge or the great pyramids of Egypt were even thought of.

From the burial chamber, the footpath continues past two small upright stones beside the fence and on down the hill. This is a well-wooded area and buzzards can often be seen circling high up above the trees, their cries a constant companion. The path passes through an open area of scattered hawthorn bushes grazed by horses, and then follows a narrow field beside the Dyffryn Gardens to where it joins a narrow lane. This is followed to the left, passing through an area of woodland in a deep cutting overhung with trees. As the lane climbs the hill, it emerges into open farmland, where a signpost points the way to the burial chamber of St Lythans, off to the right.

Standing on a gentle rise in a grassy field, the stones stand tall and dramatic. A huge weathered and hoary capstone is supported by three uprights, two of which are great wide slabs, while the third is a strange holed and pointed end stone. The rock is again mudstone, which has eroded into deep grooves and hollows and is covered in a patina of orange and grey lichen. The single chamber is as tall as it is wide which is probably the reason that it is known as Gwal-y-Filiast, 'the greyhound's kennel'. The longcairn behind the chamber is aligned east to west with the entrance to the east exactly like Tinkinswood, but it is considerably smaller.

Beyond the stone, on the crest of the rise is a strange overgrown, circular enclosure that is ringed with trees. Many legends surround this area which

The great burial chamber of Tinkinswood

allude back to its pagan past and, to this day, it is known to the locals as the 'accursed field'.

Returning to the lane at the corner of the field this is once more followed up the hill towards the village of St Lythans itself. Of interest are the number and variety of ferns which sprout from the steep banks and walls lining the road. The small village is centred on the old stone church with an unusual pitched roof to its tower. Our route follows a footpath which cuts through the churchyard and along a lane to fields where it doubles back towards the lane.

Crossing straight over, the right of way continues up a drive to an isolated house and open countryside once more. This is St Lythans Down, presumably once an area of open heathland but which is now enclosed farmland. A large tumulus, which once stood up ahead, is now sadly no more than a gentle rise in a grassy field. Our route turns left, skirts around the house and drops down towards some woodland. The path runs along just inside the edge of the wood which is mostly young birch and hazel trees, until it emerges into an area of wild scrubland at its far end. Follow the path to the left as it climbs, passes beneath a line of pylons, and drops gently down to a quiet tree-lined lane.

Turning right it is not long before a signpost is reached which points once more to Tinkinswood burial chamber. This is taken, and after crossing a wooden bridge over a small stream, it climbs back up towards the ancient site.

On my last visit, I was just beyond the stream and watching a green woodpecker as it flew lazily into a strip of woodland to the left of the path, when I noticed that beneath the trees was a 'pavement' of much weathered and moss covered stone. I looked closer and found an area of huge slabs of mudstone exactly like the stones of the burial chamber. For some reason, on this gentle rise, the bedrock was exposed, and had been split into large slabs by the natural erosion of the cracks within it. It looked very like the limestone pavements often found in the Pennines.

In places, it had been broken up and it was obvious that some of the slabs had been removed. Fascinatingly, one of the spaces matched the size and shape of the great capstone of Tinkinswood, and from it a gentle grass

St Lythans

ramp led in the direction of the longcairn. Feeling really pleased that I had found the ancient quarry site I looked more closely at the remaining slabs.

Next to the large gap was another slab of a similar size. It was deeply undercut by nature and was already partially separated from the next block by a deep but narrow crack. Irretrievably jammed into the crack was a large, wedge-shaped piece of what seemed a very different and harder rock than the local mudstone. Could I have found a stone tool, a wedge, hammered into the crack and abandoned for some unknown reason in the very process of levering away the next great block? Could it really have remained there for almost six thousand years? As it is stone, I suppose the answer is 'yes', it could well have. I certainly like to think that it has!

All around the small outcrop, hidden within its copse of hazel trees, are other stone slabs, which have been removed. Was the great cairn built here because of the proximity of this outcrop? Were the stones of St Lythans quarried here too? How did they manage to lever out and move such huge stones with only stone and wood? Many questions remain unanswered but perhaps just one more small piece of the huge jigsaw has been put into place.

From the quarry, which it must be remembered is on private land beside the path, it is just a short distance back to the longcairn. It can now be looked at in a different light, and the immense achievement of its construction can be all the better appreciated. The beginning of the walk is then retraced back to St Nicholas.

6. Trellech
Monmouth

Approx. distance: 4 miles

Approx. time: 3 hours

Starting point: Trellech, GR 501053

Grade: A short walk along quiet lanes and footpaths

O.S. Outdoor Leisure sheet: 14

Grid references: Trellech church, GR 501055; Tump Terret, GR 499054; Harold's Stones, GR 499051; The Virtuous Well, GR 503051

This is not so much a walk as a study of one of the oldest settlements in the country. The village of Trellech lies in a shallow basin, almost enclosed in the wooded hills above the Wye Valley, and has probably been lived in for at least four thousand years. For all of this time, three great stones have stood as the focal point of the community and are responsible for its name, which simply means, 'three stones'. The walk serves to put the ancient settlement into its true context within the surrounding landscape. It allows you to explore the hills above the village and look down upon it from their slopes.

When this land was first settled in Neolithic times, the whole area would have been densely forested. The Forest of Dean away to the east is now just a small remnant of the great wildwood (i.e. original forest) which once clothed all of these hills. The first farmers would have cleared land around their villages to graze their animals and grow their crops. Trellech must have been one of these places. Ideally situated in a sheltered fold in the land, it is also where a natural spring bubbled to the surface giving limitless supplies of fresh water.

Springs like this were important places to these early people who believed them to be sacred places, gifts from the great earth goddess, and as such an auspicious place to settle. There is an ancient Celtic legend that tells of when the world first began, there was no more than a single clearing in the woods, where there were three pools of water. It is just possible that this tale could date back all the way to when people lived within their own small communities, isolated and removed from the surrounding world. Just such a community could well have existed at Trellech all those years ago.

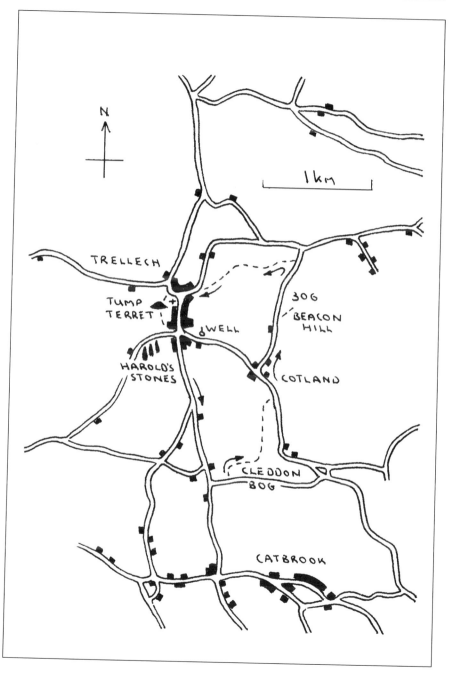

We begin the walk in the centre of the village. Where the main road leaves the last of the houses, on its way south towards Chepstow, two narrow lanes branch off to the left. Our route takes the one leading straight ahead, up the slope towards the wooded hills. As it climbs, the view out to the right stretches away beyond the nearby hills, towards the Skirrid, the sacred mountain of Gwent, and the distant Black Mountains.

The lane reaches an area of woodland covering the top of a hill known as the Broad Meend. This is not ancient woodland but a plantation of tall pines, below which is a natural regeneration of oak and birch and holly. After a left turn the nature of the woodland begins to change, the foreign pines give way to the native species of oak and ash and birch. This is the Cleddon Bog, one of the few remaining areas of old woodland left around Trellech. It has probably survived simply because it is of little use for anything else, the ground too wet and boggy to be farmed, but it serves to show us how the land around the village might once have looked.

It is a truly wild wood, with thick tangles of briars and brambles below the taller trees. Ivy clings to their trunks and spreads like a blanket across the forest floor. Beside the small stream that drains away towards the Wye valley are willows and clumps of alder, and the tussocky ground is spongy and wet. In the drier patches there are open glades of bracken with a thin scattering of birch and Scots pine. Trees rot where they fall and the wood smells of age and decay.

When I last entered the Cleddon Bog, I watched long-tailed tits and nuthatches and a woodpecker working away at a dead birch stump. I listened to siskins hidden in the pines and the rather unearthly call of an owl in broad daylight.

Our route follows a forest track, which turns off to the left and runs between the pine trees of the Broad Meend and the wilderness of the bog. Where it rejoins the lane the woods end, but still the small fields are closely hemmed in by tall, wooded hedgerows which give the feeling that they have been newly cut from the surrounding forest. In the distance, the tall spire of Trellech church can be seen ahead.

At the tiny hamlet of Cotland, another quiet lane is taken which climbs steeply up to Beacon View. This is a small car park on the edge of the large forest that blankets the hills above the Wye Gorge to the east. It offers magnificent views over the village of Trellech, lying in its hollow below, to the distant ridges and peaks of the Welsh Mountains. From Beacon View it is possible to take a footpath which climbs up through the woods to the Beacon itself, which opens up the view even more, although the actual top is now lost within the undergrowth. The strange flat-topped summit of Pen-y-Fan in the Brecon Beacons can just be seen peering over the shoulder of nearer hills.

From the viewpoint, the lane continues until a footpath turns off to the left, just before the next junction. This crosses lovely open paddocks and heads directly for the prominent spire of Trellech church. It then drops quite steeply down a rough slope, which is littered with scattered rocks and boulders of the local puddingstone. It is very likely that it was from this slope that the great stones of Trellech were originally brought. The path continues, ignoring a path off to the left, past a large old barn and heads across fields towards the church spire. After skirting around a cornfield, it finally drops down a flight of stone steps to meet a lane on the outskirts of the village.

The church is just ahead, and, although the present building is a mere 600 years old, it stands on the site of a much older Saxon church, which was built in the 7th century. In the churchyard is a curious stone pyramid and altar which probably date from this period, although the later addition of a cross on top of it suggests that it may have been an even earlier pagan structure that was later Christianised.

In the corner of the graveyard, an old stone stile leads to a footpath, running parallel to the road, and the strange mound known as the Tump Terret. This is reputed to be a medieval 'motte' or castle mound and is in fact surrounded by a defensive ditch and bank. It may well have been converted to this purpose in the Middle Ages but it is very likely that it existed thousands of years before that and was a prehistoric hill altar like those at Tomen y Faerdre and The Gop in North Wales. Evidence of its ancient provenance comes from the fact that a Roman road runs right past it, indicating that it was an important site already. There was also a local legend that evil things would happen to anyone attempting to dig into it, which is a common early-Christian superstition about ancient pagan sites. Whatever its origin it is a strange place, over forty feet high and crowned with an enormous Scot's pine tree.

The path continues through a farmyard and back to the road. The three stones of Trellech, or Harold's Stones as they are often called, are about a hundred metres away along the quite busy main road, which unfortunately has no pavement along this short section.

The stones are in a pleasant field of sheep, shielded by a high hedge from the nearby road. The first impression is one of size. The nearest is tall, the second bigger and the third is a massive leaning column of immense proportions. This giant fifteen-foot stone is at least fourteen feet around its base and appears to lean intentionally, as it enters the ground vertically. The second stone also leans, but less so, and the third is upright. They are of a local puddingstone, a conglomerate of quartz pebbles cemented solidly together. The smallest stone is smoother and more slab-like than the others and has deep erosion grooves in its top.

The strange stone altar of Trellech Church

The three stones stand in a line running roughly in a north-east to south-west alignment, and close to a tiny stream which issues from a nearby spring. The purpose of the stones is unclear. Are they fertility symbols? Do they point towards the rising of the Sun on a special day? Are they connected to the sacred spring, which is reputed to this day to have healing properties, or did they have a significance that we no longer understand? We will probably never know, but they exude such a feeling of power and importance that even I, used as I am to the wonders of the modern world, feel a sense of awe when I stand beneath them. The village has grown around them, hundreds of generations of local people have accepted them as a focal point of their community, and important features which needed to be preserved. Without this feeling of significance and attachment, there is little doubt they would have been thrown down and removed long ago.

The ancient spring can also be visited, although it is now known as St Anne's Well or the Virtuous Well, and is surrounded by a medieval wall with stone benches where the pilgrims could rest when taking the water, which is heavily laced with iron. Its medicinal properties are attributed to

Harold's Stones

Christian times but, in reality, the people of Trellech have been using its special water since long before the birth of Christ.

The exploration of the village will take as long as the walk, but is fascinating to see how the village has evolved and the ancient places have been assimilated into the way of life of later periods. The great hill altar became a fort, the sacred spring a holy well and the Christian church arose on the site of older pagan ceremonies. There is evidence of people living in Trellech from the Bronze age right through to the present day, and throughout its long history the great stones have stood, in pride of place within the settlement.

7. Merbach Hill
Hay-on-Wye

Approx. distance: 5 miles

Approx. time: 3 hours

Starting point: Bredwardine, GR 334445

Grade: A short but steep walk along well-marked paths

O.S. Explorer sheet: 201

Grid references: Merbach Hill, GR 303447; Arthur's Stone, GR 318431; Dorstone Hill, GR 327422

Between Hay-on-Wye and Hereford, the River Wye meanders in great loops across a wide, flat floodplain that curves around the lower hills of the Black Mountains. Merbach Hill is the highest of these and stands almost like a sentinel looking out over the river curling around its feet. Its gentle southern slopes were once home to a Neolithic community who built on the skyline above their settlement, a magnificent chambered tomb for their dead. This great cairn, largely denuded of its covering stones, is the main objective of our walk.

It begins in Bredwardine, a small village beside an old bridge over the river. From the main road, a narrow lane climbs steeply up onto the lower slopes of the hill. At the top of the village, a track turns off to the right and leads to a footpath which crosses small fields before opening out into pleasant parkland. This is a part of the Wye Valley walk and is well maintained and signposted. Between the tall stands of mature oak and ash trees, there are glorious views out over the Wye Valley.

The path then drops down into a mixed woodland of conifers and recently planted deciduous trees and approaches an isolated farmhouse. Before reaching it the path turns off to the left and climbs up through the woods to join a track leading steeply up to an old barn. After crossing a very muddy corner beside the barn, the path follows along the edge of the trees until the fields end and the track breaks out onto marvellous open heathland.

This is an area of bracken and scattered birch and holly trees, through which the path winds and weaves its way gently up the hill. Many magnificent, old and hoary hawthorns stand amidst dense thickets of elder and brambles and help to create a sense of wilderness far in excess of the true

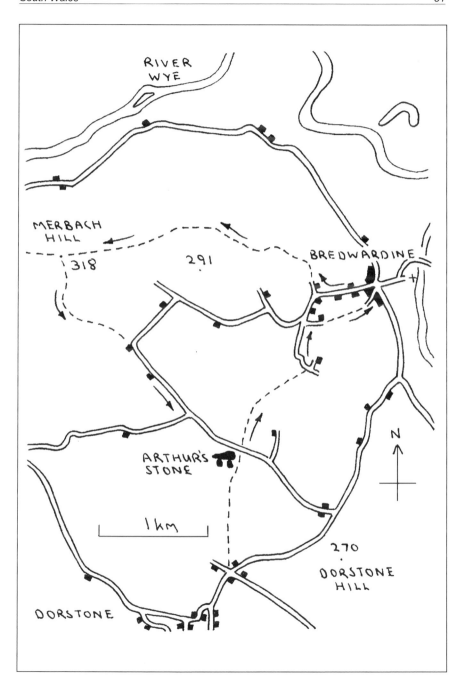

scale of the heath. On the steeper slopes to the right of the path is an area of old woodland, Westonhill Wood, where it is still possible to see how much of the area of Merbach Hill must once have looked in prehistoric times.

When the main path begins to drop back down towards the valley, a short scramble brings you quickly to the top of the hill with its panoramic views over the valleys below. To the north, beyond the snaking reaches of the River Wye, stretch the hills of the lonely borderlands of Mid Wales. To the south and west are the Black Mountains, their long dark ridges forming a sombre backdrop to the nearer wooded slopes of the 'Golden Valley' of the River Dore. This is 'God's own country', and on a clear crisp winters day it is easy to understand its well-deserved epithet. Even as long ago as 4,000 BC it must have been a desirable place to live, for it was this same view that must have inspired our Neolithic forefathers to build their place of honour to their dead ancestors. Facing towards the mid-winter setting of the sun is the great tomb of Merbach Hill, Arthur's Stone.

To reach it, a pleasant grassy path is followed along the crest of the ridge, over the strange dips and mounds of old excavations, to reach high fields and open parkland dropping gradually away to the south-east. At the edge of the first field as it falls away into the valley is a curious line of large, exposed slabs of stone, undercut and almost separated from the bedrock beneath. It is very easy to see where the great capstones of Arthur's Stone could have been found.

Beside a remote house, the path joins a lane, which provides a pleasant stroll and an ideal opportunity to admire the glorious views. Almost exactly due south, beyond the dark ridges of the Black Mountains rises the steep cone of the Skirrid, the most sacred mountain of the area, and quite possibly instrumental in the siting of the first settlements along this ridge.

Arthur's Stone stands beside the quiet lane, in its own small enclosure, and despite its mythical name, was built as much as four thousand years before King Arthur came to save the ancient Britons. It is a chambered tomb, roofed with what must once have been a capstone of immense proportions. Now broken, the two halves are still supported by an oval ring of uprights, although one tilts rather alarmingly. The smaller piece has two further slabs beneath it and it is difficult to tell if these have simply broken off the underside of the capstone or have been moved from their original site. It is possible that they once covered the entrance passage, of which only the low uprights now survive.

The large covering mound of stones has mostly gone, although the shape of the original circular cairn is clearly visible, and on one side the chambers are still partially buried. At the opposite end of the chambers to the entrance is a large isolated stone, and it is possible that this once

Arthur's Stone

blocked a false entrance into the mound. The real entrance was a low tunnel at the other end, which could easily have been covered or hidden when not in use. What is very unusual is that this entrance passage is quite long for the size of the cairn and bends at right angles before entering the burial chambers. Was this to make it harder to locate, to make it face towards the mid-winter sunset, or did the angled passage have some other significance? Another elongated burial chamber from the same period, at Locmariaquer in Brittany, also unaccountably bends at a sharp angle, although in other respects the two monuments are very different.

The question of why it was built on this spot is probably easier to answer. Some years a go, an ancient settlement site was discovered on Dorstone Hill, a flat-topped ridge of high ground just to the south-east. Flint tools, stone axeheads and pieces of Neolithic pottery were found, indicating that people were living there at the time when the Arthur's Stone burial chamber was in use. From Dorstone Hill the cairn would have been exactly on the skyline of Merbach Hill. This is no coincidence, as many of these ancient tombs were positioned carefully so that they could be clearly seen outlined against the sky when viewed from their settlements. It would seem that the juxtaposition of the earth and sky was important for the dead, possibly for spiritual reasons, or simply because the visibility kept them ever-present in the continuing life of the settlement.

Other curious aspects of the site include a cup-marked stone suppos-

The great tomb of Merbach Hill

edly found nearby, but which I have never been able to locate, and the fact that traces of a type of mortar were found between some of the stones. Not only is this very unusual in itself but it was also discovered that it contained large amounts of coal dust!

In many ways Arthur's Stone is a unique and interesting monument, but it is its situation even more that its features which make it such a wonderful place to visit. It is quiet and peaceful, the views wide and open, and although probably less wooded now, the hills still look much as they would have done all those thousands of years ago. Few people visit the site, for it is well off the beaten track, but it seems well cared for and has a sense of importance, of being an accepted and valued part of the landscape. Too many of our ancient monuments seem neglected, squashed into scruffy corners of fields or tight-ringed by rusty iron fences. Not so Arthur's Stone, for it still stands proudly on its ridge above the Golden Valley, and one gets the feeling that it might well do so for another five thousand years.

From the lane beside the stones, a footpath leads back towards Bredwardine. It crosses fields which drop gently to the corner of a small woodland, then steeply down beside the trees to reach a quiet farm track. This can be followed back over a steep-sided stream to where a footpath turns off to the right, down the hillside just before the first houses. This runs parallel to the lane and takes you pleasantly back to the main road and the centre of the village.

8. The Four Stones
Radnor Forest

Approx. distance: 9 miles

Approx. time: 5 hours

Starting point: New Radnor, GR 213608

Grade: A long walk in two halves, high wild hills followed by quiet lanes and tracks

O.S. Explorer sheet: 201

Grid references: Whimble tumulus, GR 205627; Bache Hill tumuli, GR 215636; Kinnerton standing stones, GR 245628 and, GR 246627; The Four Stones, GR 246608

New Radnor is not quite as modern as it sounds. It has sat beneath the high and brooding hills of the Radnor Forest, defended by its old town walls, for many hundreds of years. It is only when compared to the ancient landscape in which it sits, that its relatively recent place in history can be appreciated. The wide, level basin and the surrounded ring of hills, are littered with the evidence of a thriving society dating back at least four thousand years.

Among the many Bronze Age standing stones and tumuli is also one very strange and unusual site. It is a small, four-stone circle, a 'four poster', which although regularly found in northern Scotland and western Ireland are found practically nowhere else in the British Isles. Why it was built here in Mid Wales, and by whom, we shall never know, but this walk will allow you to explore the landscape and possibly discover how many of the ancient sites may be linked together.

It begins in New Radnor, a very pleasant and peaceful village dominated by a huge monument dedicated to a long-dead baronet, and follows a tiny lane that runs north into the hills of the Radnor Forest. It climbs steeply and soon reaches a dense plantation of larch and spruce blanketing the steep slope. The lane ends and a good path skirts around to the left of the woods up onto a high, open ridge.

To the south the hills of the Welsh borderland sweep away to the distant Black Mountains, while nearer at hand the ground drops away into the depths of the steep-sided valley known as Harley Dingle. Beyond it is the high plateau-land of the Forest, a bleak, heather-clad expanse of moorland rising up to a high point at Great Rhos, the 'great moor'.

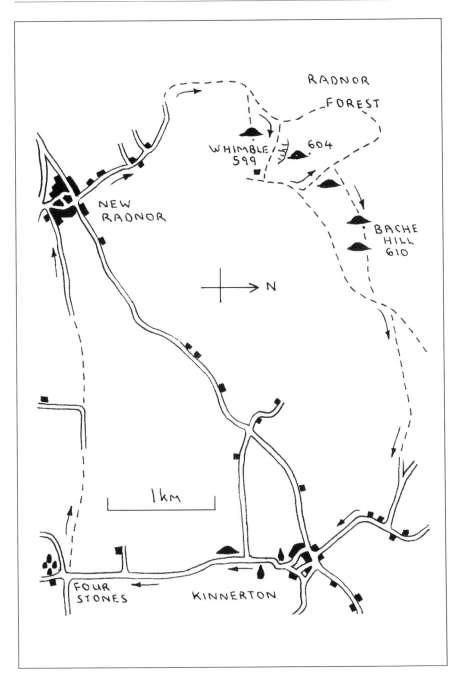

The path rises gently, passes a solitary mountain ash, and follows the edge of the plantation until the trees end and it reaches the foot of a steep conical hill rising directly above the path. This is the Whimble, which from the valley below appears as a very prominent and significant feature on the skyline. Its summit is capped by a large Bronze Age tumulus, and it is possible to scramble up a narrow path to reach it and admire the magnificent panorama it affords.

This is just the first of a line of ancient tumuli, which run along the crest of the ridge ahead forming the skyline for the lowlands below. They would, like so many others of this period, have been intentionally sited to achieve this effect. It would seem that they chose these burial sites carefully so that they appeared between the earth and the sky when viewed from their settlements. Perhaps it was thought that by so doing the souls of the dead would pass into the afterlife all the easier.

For those not wishing to climb the Whimble, the pleasant grassy path traverses easily across its lower slopes. Then a track turns off to the right, cutting through a deep gap between the Whimble and the continuation of the ridge to the north. The south-facing slopes of this pass are cut by a line of broken cliffs called Whinyard Rocks, which are formed by strange flat-topped 'turrets' of slatey rock rising from steep stony gullies. This is raven territory. They perch on the high rocks or glide and tumble over the pass, their harsh cries echoing eerily around the cliffs.

Beyond the rocks, the track joins a lane beside a large farm building. Running just above and parallel to this lane is a narrow path which can be followed until it turns steeply uphill beside the first fence, to reach the crest of the ridge. Off to the left are other large tumuli, but the route turns right over high fields to rejoin the moorland rising up to the highest point of Bache Hill, crowned by the largest of these ancient mounds.

This huge circular tumulus is over twenty paces across and still about twelve feet high. Another one, only slightly smaller, lies about a hundred metres further on. This is the last of the six tumuli that line the ridge. These great burial mounds once served the community which lived in the valley below, their position on the skyline confirming the significance that the dead still held. From the last mound a good path drops down off the hill towards the forest.

The moorland on Bache Hill is a wonderful mixture of different heathers and bilberries, and the path down allows ample opportunity to admire it. The varying hues and colours blend into a mosaic of green and brown shades moulded to the gentle contours of the land. Along the path where the heather has thinned, grasses have spread onto the moor and where the peaty soil has been exposed, there are patches of a tiny, grey

Kinnerton standing stone

lichen with bright orange horns. Rather out of place, but strikingly solitary, are several self-sown fir trees, which must have spread from the woods below.

The path joins a track which leads into the forest, but our route follows the edge of the trees, past an old copse of wonderfully twisted and entwined larch until it becomes a sunken green lane running through an avenue of gnarled hawthorns. This eventually joins a farm track and becomes a metalled lane, which drops down the hillside to the small village of Kinnerton.

After crossing the main road and passing through the cluster of old cottages, the lane comes to two small standing stones. The first is just a mossy stone lying in the grass beside the road, overgrown and easily overlooked. The second stands in the field to the left, a conical, three- to four-foot, lichen-covered stone beneath an old ash tree. Their purpose is difficult to discern, but it is possible they stood on an ancient route running down from the tumuli on the ridge towards the centre of the basin where many other Bronze Age remains can still be found. Tumuli and standing stones abound and there is an ancient pool known as the Hindwell Pool, which the Romans later thought important enough to build a fort beside.

This ancient track almost certainly ran due south from this point, roughly following the line of the modern lane. It runs as straight as an arrow towards a tall church tower in the distance. This is the church of Old Radnor, which stands on a huge prehistoric mound below Old Radnor Hill. It is no coincidence that the Four Stones and at least one burial mound stand in perfect alignment along this line.

This is the route our walk takes, passing first the site of the old tumulus, then over a low rise to reach a crossroad of lanes. Just off to the right are the Four Stones, four very large round-topped rocks standing in a small square. The largest is over six feet tall while the smallest has toppled over, away from the centre. What makes it so unusual is the size of the stones compared to the tiny central space.

As the Bronze Age wore on, the size of the stone circles shrank, as did the number of stones in them, until they reached their most simplistic form in the 'fourposters' of Scotland and Ireland. This rare Welsh example is a little gem, set in the centre of its ancient community, beneath hills capped with the burial mounds of the ancestors. Perhaps this small circle formed the focal point, the *omphalos* or 'sacred navel' of the settlement within the valley.

The stones are rough to the touch, with a strange knobbly texture and

The Four Stones of Radnor

decorated with mosses and lichens of many colours. It is possible that they were smoothed and shaped before being erected beside the old trackway.

From the Four Stones, the route takes an old green lane directly back to Old Radnor. In places it is rather wet and overgrown, but it is usually possible to avoid these sections by walking along the edge of the fields beside it. In other parts, it is a fine track running between high hedges lined with mature oak and ash trees. It crosses remote farmland and abounds in birdlife. On a winter's day finches and long-tailed tits scour the hedgerows, flocks of redwings and fieldfares sweep over the fields and dense clouds of starlings twist and circle in the sky. It runs beside the meandering Summergil Brook where herons, mallards, and grey wagtails add to the variety. The green lane eventually becomes a metalled road, which leads back into the old town.

This walk is long, but it only visits a few of the prehistoric sites in area. It was without doubt a thriving community in prehistoric times, and piecing together the scattered, but closely inter-related remains of this Bronze Age culture would take many more hours than this one walk allows. It is definitely a valley to which you will wish to return.

North Wales

The Witch Stone of Mitchell's Fold

9. Mitchell's Fold
Montgomery

Approx. distance: 7 miles

Approx. time: 4 hours

Starting point: Priestweston, GR 291974

Grade: Easy walk, but with a steep climb up Corndon Hill

O.S. Explorer sheet: 216

Grid references: Corndon Hill, GR 306969; Mitchell's Fold stone circle, GR 305984; Stapeley Hill, GR 313992; The Hoarstones, GR 324999

Hidden away in the hills which straddle the border between Shropshire and Montgomeryshire is the beautiful stone circle of Mitchell's Fold. It is at the centre of a complex group of Bronze Age sites along the line of an ancient trackway, which stretches northwards from the stone axe factory of Cwm Mawr towards the River Severn. Our walk follows a section of its route passed Corndon Hill and along the whaleback ridge of Stapeley Common.

The walk begins in Priestweston, a tiny hill village nestling under the western slopes of the hills above the valley of the River Camlad. It is a quiet place, just a few timeworn cottages and a pub beside a small stream running down from a low col in the ridge above.

The route initially follows the road south to Old Stoke Church. It is a narrow lane, winding between ancient hedgerows of oak, beech, hawthorn and holly, thickly interwoven with ivy and overhung with shrub hazels, which in February are heavy with catkins. At the first junction a lane climbs steeply up to the left and around a sharp bend to reach a low col. From there a farm track follows the ridge as it rises gently back up to the north and passes an isolated house before reaching the open fell. As you climb, the view to the west stretches to Montgomery with its hilltop castle and widens out over the plateaux and valleys of central Wales. Closer by to the south, beyond a deep and narrow valley, is the strange conical hill of Roundton.

This ridgeline is the route taken by the ancient trackway, and once out on the open hillside it begins to look very much as it must always have done. A few wind-bent hawthorns and crab-apple trees sprout from old stone banks that line the track, their gnarled trunks encrusted in moss and

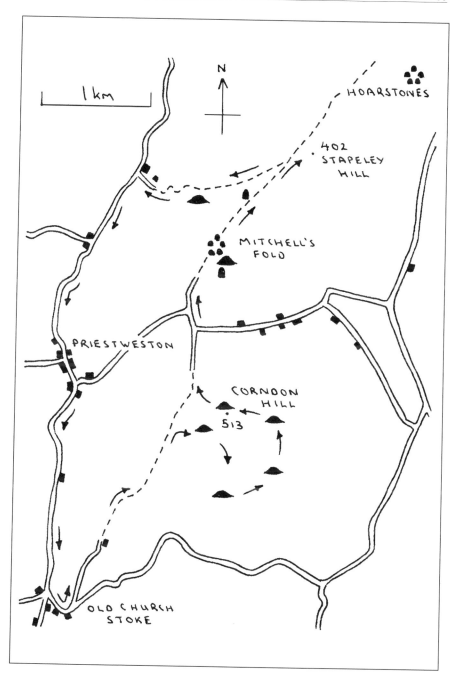

lichens. White-faced sheep graze the rough pasture and, at one place, I found two fairy rings beside the path. Buzzards circled above the wooded valley, their harsh and eerie cries carrying on the wind.

To the north, Corndon Hill with its rather disfiguring wedge of conifers, rises above the much lower but striking, rocky-topped Lan Fawr and the track rises tree-lined to a col between the two. From there, a permissive path can be taken parallel to the plantation, which climbs steeply up onto the summit plateau.

This is a special place, wide and open with panoramic views which stretch from the Long Mynd in the east to the high and lonely hills of Mid Wales fading away into the west. The top is ringed by five ancient cairns. The first is close beside the trees, now largely flattened but easily identified and beside it is a small rectangular structure whose age and purpose is unclear. The southernmost cairn sits on the crest of an outlying ridge looking out over the quiet borderlands of Shropshire. The two easternmost ones are still of enormous size, being twenty-five and twenty-seven paces across respectively, and several metres high. Both have been rearranged and windbreaks constructed on their tops, but they still manage to retain much of their original shape and form. The fifth cairn is on the summit, largely grassed over and topped by a trig point and modern cairn, but still clearly recognisable.

All of the cairns are built of the same rough blocks, probably dug from the disturbed ground still visible on the south-western slopes of the hill. They were probably built to be seen from the surrounding landscape, but equally, from the centre of the plateau they line the edge of the near horizon, adding to the unique atmosphere of this high and lonely place. Its very name Corndon is quite likely a derivation of 'cairndon' or 'cairn-topped'.

The main bridleway can be rejoined by a steep path down the other side of the belt of trees. This is then followed northwards towards where a quiet road crosses over the ridge. In the last field on the right, a stone circle known as the Whetstones once stood. It has now gone, and the large stones forming the far boundary of the field are probably all that remain of it. Fortunately, the next circle at Mitchell's Fold has survived and crowns the crest of the ridge ahead.

To reach it the route crosses the road and the national boundary, and takes a lane running up towards Stapeley Hill. As the lane ends, a path continues over beautiful sheep-cropped open heathland which rises to the high and wide plateau on which sits the circle.

In fact it is not a circle at all, but an ellipse, about thirty paces across at its widest. Most of the stones are small, and many are missing or fallen, but the largest of the fifteen that remain is a fine dramatic blade of rock known

Mitchell's Fold stone circle beneath Stapeley Hill

as the Witch's Stone. It is over six feet high and wonderfully decorated with tiny mosses and lichens. It is probable that, like all the other known circles in the area, this one once had a central stone, but no evidence of this survives. More than the stones themselves, it is their position that makes them special. This high heathland is far removed from the modern world and the views are little changed from when the stones were first dragged from the nearby hilltop and raised on this lonely ridge.

On the slight rise above the ring to the south-east are the remains of a Bronze Age cairn, although only a few of the larger kerb stones are still visible above the grass and the bracken. Just beyond it is a small outlying standing stone and beyond that once stood another one, now sadly destroyed. It is possible that they were part of a line of stones, which once ran along the ridge marking the line of the trackway, or even an avenue of paired stones linking the circles together.

Bronze axe heads and stone hammer-axes from Cwm Mawr have been discovered at the circle, again evidence of the importance of the trade that flowed along this ancient route.

Beyond the circle the land climbs gently and, several hundred metres further along, the path passes a large fallen standing stone on a low rise. Above it, the shapely top of Stapeley Hill rises to the right of the path and it is an easy climb up the steepening slopes to its rocky cairn. The direct line follows a line of stone blocks partially buried beneath the grass. Its long summit ridge is a delightful place to sit and take in the surrounding scenery. To the east the rocky outcrops of the Stiperstones stand out clearly on the horizon, and nearer at hand the line of the ancient trackway can easily be made out snaking away along the ridge before dropping away to the north.

It is possible to extend the walk for a further mile, down to where the third circle, called the Hoarstones, still stands on an uncultivated island in a quiet field beyond the far end of the ridge. It is of a similar size to Mitchell's Fold, but has many closely-spaced small stones surrounding its large central stone. This fine stone is beautifully encrusted with yellow lichen. Another stone hammer-axe was also discovered here, adding to the likelihood that they were buried intentionally within the circles as an offering or gift to the spirits.

Instead of continuing further however, our route turns back to the west, returning to the track and crossing it along another path, which climbs up and over a low outlying ridge, before dropping steeply down to meet a tiny

The Hoarstones

lane. Several ancient mounds marked on the map beside this path are very difficult to locate beneath the bracken. The lane is easily followed to the road which winds its way uneventfully back, between high hedges to Priestweston.

On Stapeley Hill the once rich legacy of our ancestors has been much damaged and despoiled over the passing centuries, but fortunately enough has survived for us to recreate the ancient landscape in our minds. Imagine a hill crowned with a ring of great cairns. Below it, a trackway weaves along a high open ridge of heather and bracken above densely wooded valleys. A stone circle stands at each end, and a third, the greatest of the three, on its broad crest. Beside it, a large cairn rises from a low hill and a line of standing stones runs along the skyline between the circles. Then, as now, this must have been a magical and mystical place.

10. Pistyll Rhaeadr Llanrhaeadr-ym-Mochnant

Approx. distance: 6 miles

Approx. time: 4-5 hours

Starting point: Pistyll Rhaeadr, GR 077294

Grade: A high mountain walk crossing wild and remote moorland

O.S. Explorer sheet: 255

Grid references: Pystyll Rhaeadr, GR 073295; 'Old Man' of Berwyn, GR 072324; Cadair Berwyn, GR 073327; stone circle, GR 057302; stone row, GR 058302; cairn circle, GR 059303

This is not an easy walk. In places it is difficult underfoot and is best avoided after periods of prolonged wet weather. Nor is the navigation straightforward, as the only paths in the second half of the walk are those made by the few sheep that graze these wild uplands. In low cloud and poor visibility it becomes more than a simple walk and takes on a more serious mantle requiring experience and understanding of map and compass. Despite this, or perhaps because of this, it is a magnificent day out and provides a unique opportunity to discover and explore a fascinating Bronze Age complex almost hidden away in an unspoiled and little-visited wilderness.

The walk begins below Pistyll Rhaeadr, the spectacular waterfall which is justly counted as one of the seven wonders of Wales. It is approached along a narrow lane from Llanrhaeadr-ym-Mochnant, which ends just a short walk away from its foot. Draining the vast uplands beyond, the Afon Disgynfa plunges almost two hundred feet into a deep circular pool, flows out through a natural arch and fall again about sixty feet to the bottom of the gorge. On either side of the fall, the near vertical cliffs are draped in luxuriant vegetation more reminiscent of a tropical rainforest than a Welsh hillside.

For hundreds of years, visitors have stared up at the fall, and now a newly constructed path makes the route to its top much easier, but few get far beyond it. A belt of dense scrub and woodland surrounds the small clearing, and steep rock steps above the fall hide the true extent of the landscape beyond. For, stretching away for miles, is the largest tract of open moorland in Wales.

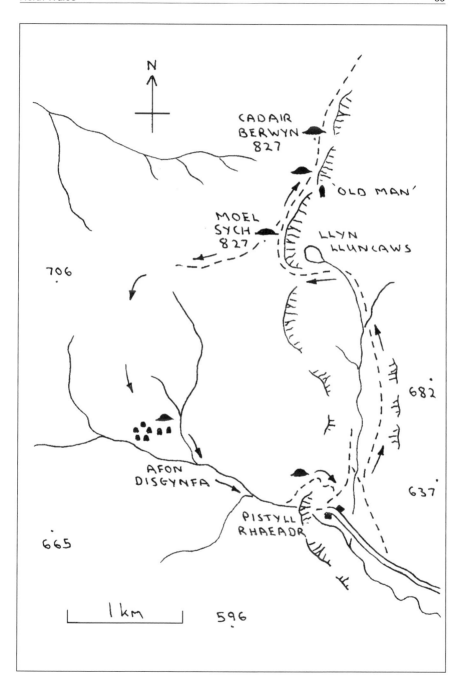

Shaped by tumbling streams, which have cut into the high plateau, the moors rise up to a long ridge crowned by the twin summits of Moel Sych and Cadair Berwyn. The whole landscape is a giant sponge which feeds the headwaters of the two great rivers of Wales, the Dee and the Severn, and ensure that the tumbling waters of Pistyll Rhaeadr never dry up.

It would be impossible to start the walk without first making the short journey to stand in the spray beneath the fall and admire its magnificent natural architecture. Then, by following signs for the top of the waterfall, a path can be followed through the woods, passing between tall and elegant beech trees, which stand like sentinels guarding the valley beyond. Ignoring the steep path up to the fall, continue instead up into the side valley until it is possible to cross the tumbling stream and climb up to the obvious track running along the far side of the valley.

Within minutes, the shadowy and enclosed main valley is left behind and ahead the side valley sweeps up towards high ridges topped with broken cliffs. The track is grassy and easy underfoot, climbing gently across a hillside of sheep-nibbled heather and bilberries, interspersed with taller patches of dark green ferns. Grey scree slopes fan out beneath the broken crags above, in parts overgrown with bright yellow splashes of gorse. On a calm day late one summer, I walked up here with a friend and watched stonechats balancing precariously on the topmost sprigs of the gorse and ravens tumble and dive, black against the grey rocks above.

The path steepens and climbs beside the stream to reach the waters of Llyn Lluncaws, hidden away in a fold of the hills beneath the rocky slopes falling steeply from the main ridge. From the lake, the path turns upwards, following the rounded ridge which climbs quickly towards the skyline. As it nears the top it runs along the very lip of the crags giving an exciting view back down to the lake nestling in its hollow directly below. Away to the right, on the rocky crest of the summit ridge the small pinnacle known as the 'Old Man of Berwyn' stands out clearly.

Before long, the path opens out onto the broad summit ridge, which is easily followed, past a tiny memorial, onto the rocky outcrop above the 'Old Man'. The views are magnificent. To the east, low hills drop away towards England, but to the west all the mountain ranges of North Wales stand in line. The Arans, the Rhinogs, the Arenigs, Snowdon itself, the Glyders and the Carneddau ring the horizon beneath a vast dome of sky. Away to the north is the sea, sparkling between the rounded hills of Clwyd and the wild moorlands of Denbighshire.

On one occasion, as I sat sheltering from the wind beside the small pinnacle, a peregrine falcon flashed past me skimming soundlessly over the rocks before dropping like an arrow into the valley below.

The 'Old man' of Berwyn

Between the rocks and the actual summit is a huge ancient cairn, now shaped into a wind shelter, and the trig point itself sits upon another. With a third and fourth crowning the tops of nearby Cadair Bronwen and Moel Sych, and others at prominent places along the ridge, these cairns must have been visible for miles, marking this as a place of considerable significance in ancient times.

From Cadair Berwyn the route is retraced to Moel Sych, and it is here that the whole aspect of the walk changes. A signpost points the way towards a distant Milltir Gerrig, but the path vanishes. The pleasant sheep-cropped turf is replaced with rough heather and bilberry and open expanses of peat. As the ridge drops it broadens to become a wide plateau cut through with sticky peat hags and dotted with deep pools of iridescent green water. Red grouse clatter away as if surprised at the unexpected intrusion. All that remains to remind you of the present is a fence which, before long, drops away into the valley to the left. Ahead the moor sweeps on, bleak and unbroken, into the distance.

At this point, our route also turns to the left, following a rounded spur of land dropping down between two side valleys, towards the main valley of the Afon Disgynfa. This is rough country, with areas of tussock grass interspersed with reeds and heather. Below, on a level terrace above the main valley, is the strange complex of megalithic sites that is the prime reason for this walk.

From above it is invisible, just a sweep of wild moorland mottled with patches of reeds and ferns. In fact, it is not until you actually arrive at the site, and that is a challenge in itself, that the stones appear, scattered and half hidden within the vegetation. If it had not been for my friend stumbling over the kerb stones of a burial cairn, we might have missed it altogether.

Once located, it is fascinating to piece together the pieces of the jigsaw. A tiny but complete stone circle of fifteen small stones, surrounding a single rounded, central stone, sits on a low rise. From it, two parallel lines of stones about three paces apart stretch for about eighty metres in the rough direction of, but not directly at, a small kerbed cairn. Nowhere do the stones stand more than three feet high, many are missing and some barely rise above the surrounding vegetation, but this only adds to the wildness of the site. It is fascinating to part the fern fronds to find a stone exactly where you expect it to be. It allows a sense of discovery and exploration that is so rare in today's well-documented world. Perhaps more still remains to be discovered in this wild and lonely valley.

The parallel stone rows are a real mystery. Similar ones are found on Dartmoor, but they are rare elsewhere, and these are the only examples that I know of in Wales. Did they form a ceremonial avenue along which people approached the stone circle? Were they smaller versions of the great avenues of Avebury? Did they once link the circle to the burial cairn, connecting in some way, the ancestors with the continuing cycle of life? All answers are possible, but we will probably never know the true purpose of these ancient lines drawn across the moor.

It seems so easy to let time drift by in this fascinating place, trying to piece together the remaining clues to imagine the valley as it once was, but eventually a return to the 21st century will be necessary. The easiest route is to drop down into the side valley called Cwm Rhiwiau and cross the stream above where it cuts down into a deep wooded gorge. Just beyond the stream is a narrow path, which winds its way through the ferns to reach the main river beside the ruins of an old settlement.

On the far side of the river, which can be crossed easily at this point, is a

The elusive stone circle of the Afon Disgynfa

gate that leads to a faint path running along beside the water. In places the path seems to vanish completely only to reappear again further on. As the river begins to drop more steeply, the vegetation becomes thicker and taller and further progress becomes difficult. There is a path, which recrosses the stream and skirts around the woodland to the left, but it is difficult to find. Instead it seems more in keeping with the nature of the walk to battle on through the ferns, into the trees and to follow the river as it tumbles over small falls and down spectacular waterslides to reach the top of the main waterfall.

Here, just beneath a natural rock shelter, the water leaps out into space. Only by leaning out rather precariously on an old birch tree overhanging the drop, is it possible to look down and see just how dramatic the fall really is. This greatest of natural features must have been well known and was almost certainly sanctified as a holy place from the earliest of times. The people who built the strange stone rows must surely have sat and wondered at the faint rainbows shimmering in the spray rising from the fall.

The well-signposted path back down climbs first up onto the open hillside before descending steeply down a zigzag path to the café and the car park. It is obvious, easily followed, and provides a pleasant but rather tame ending to a wild and wonderful walk.

11. Moel Ty-uchaf
Llandrillo

Approx. distance: 4 miles

Approx. time: 2 hours 30 mins

Starting point: Llandrillo, GR 035372

Grade: Short but steep walk on the edge of wild hills

O.S. Explorer sheet: 255

Grid references: Moel Ty-uchaf circle, GR 056372; Tyfos circle, GR 028387; Rhydyglafes chambered cairn, GR 047396

The lonely heather-clad ridges of the Berwyn Mountains rise wild and remote above the wide valley of the River Dee. Like great waves the high tops of Moel Sych and Cadair Berwyn rear up to form cliffs, towering above their long eastern valleys. To the west, the more gentle slopes are cut by shorter, steep-sided valleys. Between two of these, and on the end of a long spur of high ground, is the rounded hill of Moel Ty-uchaf, 'the hill of the highest house'. On its top is a small but beautiful stone circle.

To reach it, our walk begins in Llandrillo, a small town on either side of an old bridge over the River Ceidiog, just above where it joins the deeper waters of the Dee. A tiny lane leaves the main road beside a chapel and climbs steeply up the hillside to where it becomes a rough farm track running through an area of old oak and birch woodland. Shadowed by the dense foliage, an enormous moss-covered boulder lies just to the right of the track.

As it leaves the woodland, the route enters an area of open grassland scattered with thickets of gorse and hawthorn trees. Away to the west, the wide valley of the Dee weaves between low wooded hills, and beyond it range upon range of hills fade away into the distance. Another huge pock-marked and lichen-covered rock sits close beside a line of old ash trees to the left of the path. Just past this huge stone, the track enters a shallow valley with a stream, which is crossed on tiny stepping stones.

Beyond the stream, the track becomes lined with large boulders and tangled thickets of coconut-scented gorse. After a second stream it widens out and runs between ancient stone banks. At one point a line of large stones, equally spaced, sit within the bank possibly indicating that they are from an earlier period.

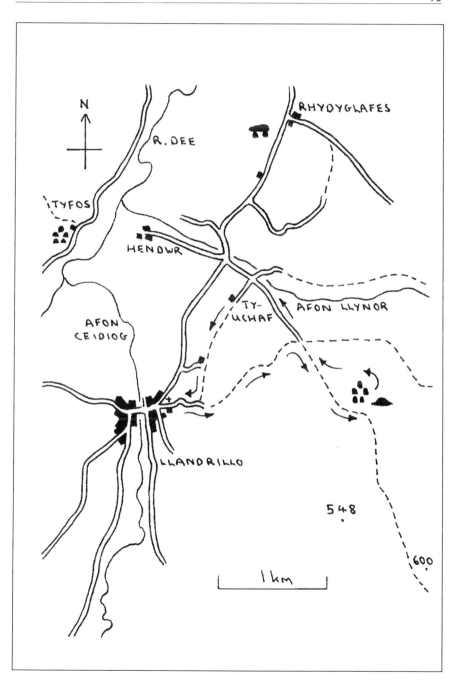

Standing beside these old stones it is possible to look down and across to the far bank of the River Dee to a white house at the foot of a narrow wooded valley. Close to this house are the remains of the large cairn circle of Tyfos. Running through the wooded valley and past the circle to the river, was an ancient prehistoric trackway. Coming from the Conwy Valley and the important settlement areas of the north coast, this trackway once crossed the river below Tyfos, probably at a small ferry. From there, it climbed up the hillside, along the line of the lane, which is just ahead, towards the pass of Bwlch Maen Gwynedd over the Berwyn Mountains. This high pass is marked by ancient cairns, the one on the highest point being of pure white quartz. Beyond the pass, the trackway drops down to the valleys and gentler countryside of Mid Wales.

Just beyond this vantage point you come to a crossroads where the path meets the lane which follows the line of the ancient trackway. Turning right you begin to follow this early routeway as it becomes a track climbing up towards the distant mountains. How many thousands of years ago did people first tread this ancient route? Did they use it to trade with distant settlements, did they carry with them axes and blades from the great axe factory at Craiglwyd to the north or were they merely driving their animals to fresh pasture beyond the hills? It was probably used for all these purposes, and many more.

We know that some of the ancient circles and burial chambers of Wales take the form of those in Ireland, as does the art carved into many of their stones. We know that some chambers are similar to those of the Cotswolds and Wiltshire and some even show characteristics of those in Brittany. We know that axes from Wales have been discovered all over the country. From all this evidence, we must assume that people and their ideas and customs moved freely throughout the land, crossing seas and mountains, and that these trackways were vital in the development and success of their society. It is fascinating to imagine it as it must once have been, a major route linking important but scattered areas of settlement together.

To the left of the track is the rounded hill of Moel Ty-uchaf, but it is not until you almost reach its top that the circle comes into view as a line of low stones. Even then, it is not until you actually reach it that it is revealed as a complete and almost contiguous stone ring. Part of the magic of its position is that everywhere can be seen from it, but that it is hidden from view from all directions until it is actually arrived at.

It is a beautiful circle in a wonderful setting. The Arans, the Arenigs and the Carneddau ring the horizon and cradled between their high ridges is the great basin of the upper Dee. Just visible, peering over the shoulders of the nearer peaks are the distant Rhinogs, rising in isolation away to the

Moel Ty-uchaf stone circle looking towards the Arenigs

west. Closer at hand, Cadair Bronwen, itself topped by an ancient cairn, stands above a belt of trees to the south-east.

The circle is made of forty touching stones and is about twelve paces across. It has two gaps, to the east and south-east, one of which might have been an entrance. All the stones are small, although slightly larger ones are separated by smaller ones at regular intervals. In the centre are the remains of a small burial cist. It is possible that an original circle of larger stones was later changed into a contiguous ring when the internal burial cairn was added.

Just below the circle to the south-east are the remnants of another kerbed cairn. Little remains except a few of the kerbs and some smaller stones showing through the rough grass. What is noticeable, however, is that the stones that are visible are all of white quartz, just like the cairn on the summit of the pass through the mountains. What a spectacular sight these cairns must have been thousands of years ago!

Returning to the circle it is well worth continuing along the line of the hill top, if only for the magnificent views away to the west. This is also the only direction from which the circle can be viewed from any distance at all, allowing it to be seen in the context of the surrounding landscape.

After a short distance, a fence-line runs across the hill, but it is possible

The touching stones of Moel ty-uchaf

to circle back down to rejoin the track rather than simply retracing your steps. At the crossroads, the direct route downhill is taken, following the line of the prehistoric trackway. This becomes a steep and narrow lane running straight down the slope. This ancient route is deeply incised below the level of the fields, and the high banks are lined with old oak and ash trees. Behind the hedge to the left is a line of large rounded boulders which have probably just been cleared from the surrounding fields but which add a certain feeling of importance and significance to the route. In spring, the banks are thick with wild flowers, primroses and violets, celandines and bluebells and the tiny white stars of the stitchwort shine out from the hedgerows.

The trackway would have continued on, down to the main road, past a very old barn and down towards the river, to a crossing beside the house of Hendwr, meaning 'old water'. Our route, however, turns off to the left, along a private road but public footpath, towards the farm of Ty-uchaf.

The steep field to the left is marked by three huge blocks of stone, too big to have ever been cleared away. The road ends at the farm, but a track turns off beside a small pool ringed with delicate, lilac cuckoo flowers towards some animal pens. A small metal gate allows access to a field, beyond which is a stream that can be crossed by a 'clapper bridge' – one made from a single slab of stone. This leads to more fields, scattered with blocks of stone and dense patches of bracken and hawthorn. The path here is well marked by stiles as it climbs above another farmhouse to rejoin the steep lane dropping back down to Llandrillo.

This is a short walk and the stone circle is all that remains to be seen of the prehistory of the area. Other sites still exist nearby, the circle at Tyfos, several ruined burial chambers and many prehistoric cairns and tumuli scattered throughout the mountains. This walk is merely an introduction to this fascinating and historically important area.

12. Tomen y Faerdre Llanarmon-yn-Ial

Approx. distance: 5 miles

Approx. time: 3 hours

Starting point: Llanarmon-yn-Ial, GR 190562

Grade: Straightforward walk over high hills

O.S. Explorer sheet: 265

Grid references: Moel y Plas, GR 170555; Tomen y Faerdre, GR 193562

On the eastern side of the great Clwydian range runs the River Alyn. Beside the river on a low rise, and below the prominent domed hill of Moel y Plas is the village of Llanarmon-yn-Ial. It is an ancient place that has probably been inhabited for at least five thousand years and was very likely a site of sacred importance long before that. Further along the valley to the south near the farm at Rhos Isaf, 'the lowest moor', are caves which have yielded many finds including human burials, early pottery, stone tools and the bones of many wild animals.

To the hunter-gatherers of the Mesolithic Period who lived a largely nomadic existence, certain natural features would have come to play an important role in their lives. These were places that were easily recognisable and gave structure to their transitory lifestyle. Prominent hills, natural springs, caves or great rocks became significant places and eventually some would have developed into sites of ritual importance. Here at Llanarmon, at an obvious crossing point of the river is a large cave and a huge natural outcrop of limestone, both looking up towards the distant summit of Moel y Plas. It is hardly surprising that it became an important site and it was here that the later Neolithic people chose to build a great cairn and stone circle.

When I last walked this route it was a marvellous, crisp day in January with the snow lying deep in the folds of the mountains and a pale winter sun casting long shadows over the frozen fields. The trees and fenceposts were decorated with shining crystals of frost, and in the sky a pair of buzzards circled high and silent above a small patch of woodland beside the river.

The walk starts in the centre of the village beside the church and takes

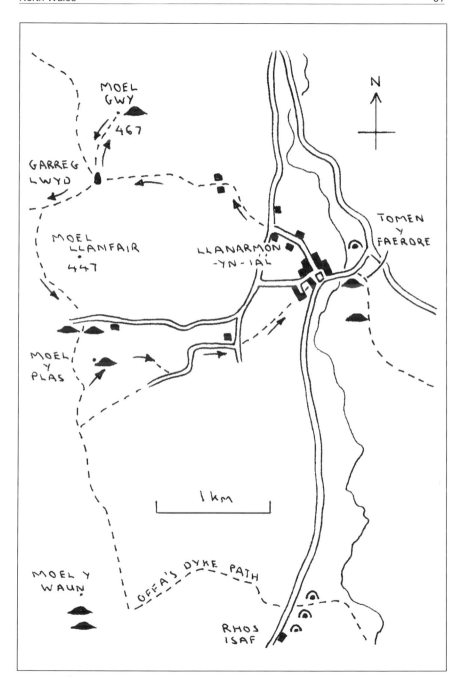

the narrow lane called Ffordd Rhiw Ial out to the north. At the first road junction, and beside a large chapel a footpath leads up and over the brow of the hill to join a farm track leading to the farm of Banhadlan Ganol. The path skirts around it and over a tiny stream before climbing steeply up, past a last, isolated house to reach a high field. At its top, a line of stunted and wind-shaped hawthorn and ash trees marks the beginning of the open hillside.

Climb up to the ridgeline where the already extensive view broadens out and stretches from the coastlands to the north to the distant peaks of Llantysilio Mountain away to the south. Much nearer is Moel y Plas, changed now from the steep conical shape it takes when viewed from Llanarmon, to a long whaleback stretching out from the main line of the hills. The ridge climbs gently upwards to reach the high col of Garreg Lwyd which, as its name implies, is marked by a single large rock at its lowest point. As you reach it an enormous view opens up to the west, across the wide Vale of Clwyd to the Denbigh Moors, and above them the sharp peaks of Snowdonia hang on the distant horizon.

Above the col the ridge continues up to the north towards the summit of Moel Gyw and a good path can be followed through the now rougher vegetation of heather, bilberry and stunted gorse to its top. Just beyond the trig point is a small ancient tumulus looking out to the east and from where Llanarmon is clearly visible in the valley below. Having admired the view it is necessary to return to the col and join the Offa's Dyke path which drops down and around Moel Llanfair along an excellent track, easy underfoot and with the extensive view to the west a delightful and constant companion.

It was on this section that I watched three ravens, jet black against the pale sky, soar up over the snowfields before tumbling down into a steep and narrow valley, only breaking their fall at the very last minute. Then a few quick wing beats carried them up and over the ridge to glide effortlessly away into the distance on upcurled wings.

This track soon brings you to a narrow lane which crosses over the range at a low col. On the far side of the lane are two Bronze Age tumuli, one grass-covered in a field and the other on the open moor and clad in heather and bilberry. They mark the high point of the pass, indicating that this was an important crossing point in ancient times.

Above the tumuli, the path climbs quickly up onto the shoulder of Moel y Plas, passing below the summit, until a stile allows you to cross the fence and climb up to the top. This sacred site is also marked with its own small tumulus crowned with a modern cairn, although the hill would probably have been revered from afar long before the mound was erected in the

A lost stone of Llanarmon-yn-Ial

Bronze Age. From the top of the cairn it is just possible to see the church in Llanarmon and the site of the Tomen y Faerdre, and the route down follows almost exactly the line of an ancient trackway which would once have linked the hill with the settlement.

Head straight down the ridge to the east, until it drops steeply down to a belt of trees which is split by a path leading to a lane. This is followed down the ridge, in places cut deep below the level of the fields by millennia of use, to reach the road as it levels out onto the valley floor. Crossing the road another footpath leads straight towards the church, crossing fields and a small new housing estate before arriving at its western gate.

In Neolithic times this was the site of a great stone circle, built on a low rise above the river and the great natural rock outcrop beside the ancient trackway running along the valley. Little of the circle remains, except its shape mirrored in the circular graveyard and a number of its ancient stones

Tomen y Faerdre

which can still be found around the church, now used as gateposts or dumped unceremoniously out of the way. One such stone can be easily located just beside the stile as the path meets the road beside the church.

It was common practice in the early days of Christianity to build churches on the sites of the more ancient religions, but whether this was an act of dominance and replacement, or merely an indication of the continuing significance of the sites is still unclear. In many instances the stones were left, hinting at a blending of the old and new religions, possibly by people who retained much of the pagan in their lives.

Beyond the church the road continues on a direct alignment from the hill through the church to where the great Tomen y Faerdre rises above the river crossing. This great natural outcrop of limestone is capped by a huge Neolithic cairn built of small rough stones. This is, in fact, a miniature

Silbury, a great man-made altar created in the image of the mother mountain in the distance. The cairn is surrounded by a ditch and an outer bank, except where the river cuts into the steep northern face. This rather discounts the theory that these were added in medieval times to create a fort, as the ditch would have been outside the bank had its purpose been defensive.

As I stood on the top of the enormous mound, away to the west through the trees which now grow on its steep flanks rose the snow-covered Moel y Plas, dominating the skyline and I could easily understand how one must have inspired the other.

Beyond the tomen, further along the farm track and on the top of the low hill, lies another known as Tomen Kefrydd and two more, smaller mounds can still be found about a hundred metres away to the south-west above the steep slopes of the river. A local name, Bwlch Crug-Glas or 'pass of the green mounds', no doubt refers to these ancient cairns.

Llanarmon-yn-Ial is truly a settlement of prehistoric origins, which can be visited easily by car. But to fully appreciate the significance of the site, walk up into the high hills to the west, stand on the top of Moel y Plas and picture the landscape as it once was, then drop down along the trackway into the village before searching for the remaining clues to its unique and ancient heritage.

13. The Gop
Prestatyn

Approx. distance: 6 miles

Approx. time: 3 hours 30 mins

Starting point: Llanasa, GR 106814

Grade: Easy walking over gentle hills and along quiet lanes

O.S. Explorer sheet: 265

Grid references: The Gop, GR 086802; Gop Caves, GR 086801; St Elmo's Summer House, GR 085817

Above the flat and populated coastal plain of North Wales where the estuary of the River Dee meets the Irish Sea, is an undulating limestone plateau of low wooded hills and quiet farms. It is an ancient landscape, criss-crossed with early trackways and dotted with cairns and tumuli from prehistoric times. On a high hill, now largely shielded by trees, but once visible for miles in all directions, is the Gop. Hidden by its modern plantation and largely by-passed by all but the occasional walker, this great monument sits quietly on its hilltop and looks out over a landscape little changed by the passing centuries. With the exception of Silbury Hill in Wiltshire, this great Neolithic cairn is probably the largest prehistoric, man-made structure in the whole of Europe!

Our walk begins in Llanasa, a beautiful village of stone cottages surrounding an old church, which nestles in a shallow valley between low green hills. It takes the lane to the south which climbs up the hill, until a right fork followed by a right and left turn down very narrow lanes brings you to the brow of the hill. As you climb, the view behind you to the north-east opens up across the sands of the Dee Estuary to Hilbre Island and the Wirral Peninsula.

In the field immediately to the right are two Bronze Age circular barrows, now no more than low grassy mounds cresting the broad ridge. The path passes them, skirts an area of disturbed, strangely hummocky ground to join a tiny lane. A left turn through a quiet farmyard leads to a path, which drops down to the road. In the field opposite is another barrow, again on high ground leading up towards Gop Hill, now close by to the west.

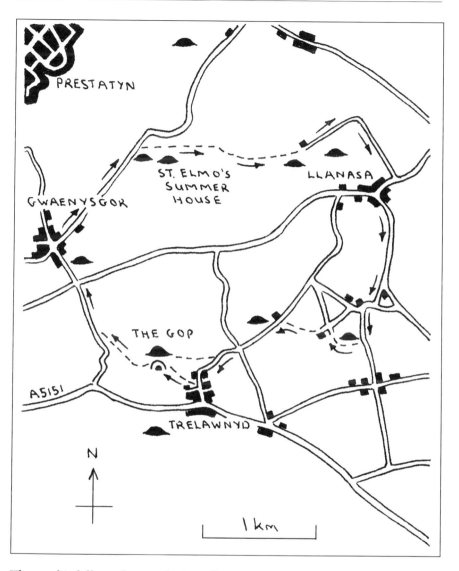

The road is followed towards the village of Trelawnyd until a signpost indicates a new millennium footpath leading into the woods and onto the hilltop. This can be easily followed to the Gop, but better still, continue down into the village where a short side lane and a stile leads onto the open south-facing slopes.

The path up the hill passes one of the ancient quarries where much of the limestone for the great cairn was dug out of the hillside. It was only when I stood below these manmade cliffs for the first time that I began to appreciate the enormity of the task that faced the people who decided to build this huge altar on the hilltop. Lacking all metal, the rock would have been prised loose from the bedrock using only tools made from stone, bone and wood. They must have worked away with deer antler picks and levers made of fire-hardened staves and driven wooden wedges into the cracks with stone hammers to break off large blocks of stone. Then they would have dragged the blocks, probably using sledges, up the steep slopes to the top where they were to be used.

Follow the route they would have taken towards the cairn, which gradually comes into view. Around its base grows a dense thicket of undergrowth, but the path weaves through it to where a ring of huge kerbstones once ringed the mound. Some can still just be seen, but most have fallen or have been covered as time and old excavations have worn away at the original shape and size of the cairn.

Each time I climb by the faint track which spirals up to the top, I am still stunned by the breathtaking view in all directions which awaits me. To the north, the sea shimmers beyond the nearer hills and, to the east, the Dee Estuary and the level plains of England fade into the distance. To the south, the great Clwydian ridge rises, hill beyond hill, to the great mother mountain, Moel Famau and to the west on the far horizon, beyond the distant moors, the snow-flecked peaks of Snowdonia edge the horizon.

The size of the cairn is still truly remarkable. Despite the passing millennia and the great crater-like hollow in the summit it is still at least twenty metres high and its base about fifty metres across. What beliefs drove its makers to raise such a monument? What rituals were carried out on its high, levelled top? Like the few other such ancient structures to have survived, no burials have ever been found beneath or within them to explain their purpose. Perhaps it is the mystery that adds to the atmosphere, but to stand alone on its summit and look out over the vast and ancient landscape is an experience to be treasured.

Dropping down from the cairn, and immediately below it to the south, are the Gop Caves, several low, natural caverns in the limestone. These caves were known and used well before the cairn was erected on the hilltop above.

Such natural features had become more than just places of temporary shelter, for they entered into the very bowels of the earth and were seen as entry points to another world. The cool, damp atmosphere, the echoes and the distortion of sounds and the darkness, all added to the sense of unworldliness, and created in the minds of the people a belief that these

The Gop

were places to be revered. Prehistoric burials have been found here and it is very likely that these caves were the precursors of the cairn above, built on an already sacred site. One is large enough to enter easily, and with the help of a torch, it is possible to climb into and sit inside a small but comfortable chamber. It would be difficult to sit within it and not be aware of the enormous passage of time and sense the legacy of events, which must once have taken place on this ancient hill.

From the caves the route crosses the open hillside, and drops down across fields to a road, which takes you into the picturesque village of Gwaenysgor. Here you will find another of those Welsh circular churchyards indicating a history which predates the Christian church at its centre, and close by a natural spring.

From the crossroads in the middle of the village, you take the narrow lane running north-east which rises towards the crest of a low ridge of hills blocking the view to the coast. As you gain height it is fascinating to watch the top of The Gop gradually appear over the trees on its hilltop to the south. Just after the road reaches its highpoint, a footpath turns off to the right and in the first field are two more Bronze-Age barrows.

The first, close by the road, is low and indistinct, but the second, which

The 'sacred' caves of The Gop

sits in a magnificent position on the very top of the hill, is a well-preserved example of a large tumulus surrounded by a ditch and outer bank. The bank is constructed of loose stone, largely grassed over but with several larger stones still visible. Unfortunately the top of the barrow itself has been levelled off in more recent times and has had a concrete and brick building erected upon it. This has been largely removed but rubble from it is still visible in the ditch. It also suffers from the rather fanciful name of St Elmo's Summer House! Despite these blemishes, it retains much of its original shape and its position and size indicate a site that must have been of great importance in its time.

The path follows the edge of a belt of woodland, and on across fields to reach a small pool almost surrounded by undergrowth. This is high and wild farmland. There are dense thickets of gorse where stonechats flit from bush to bush, and as you approach, flocks of lapwings burst into flight and wheel noisily away over the hills. A line of windswept trees and stunted hawthorns raise their heads above the banks and hedgerows, and beyond it all, the vast and empty seascape to the north constantly draws the eye.

From the pool, a track drops gradually down to the east passing two more barrows on the way. The first is just a rise of rough grass in a cabbage field and the second a grassy hump in a field of sheep. The track becomes a lane, and the lane becomes a road, which soon turns south and brings you pleasantly and easily back to Llanasa.

14. Capel Garmon Betws-y-coed

Approx. distance: 7 miles

Approx. time: 3 hours 30 mins

Starting point: Capel Garmon, GR 816555

Grade: Easy walk along quiet lanes, farm tracks and well-marked footpaths

O.S. Outdoor Leisure sheets: 17 and 18

Grid references: Maen Pebyll long barrow, GR 844566; Capel Garmon chambered long cairn, GR 818543

Just to the north-east of where the Afon Conway tumbles over the Conway Falls and winds through the Fairy Glen is an area steeped in ancient history. It is a land of rolling hills and shallow valleys climbing up from the narrow gorge of the Conway to the bleak hills of the Denbigh Moors. Small remnants of old woodland still cling to the steeper hillsides, but in the main this is sheep country, with broken walls and old hedgerows criss-crossing the land.

At its heart is the village of Capel Garmon, just a pleasant inn, a fine chapel and a small cluster of houses tucked away in the folds of the green hills. Nearby is the celebrated Neolithic chambered cairn of the same name, a fine testimony to the thousands of years of human history, which has been etched into this ancient landscape.

Our walk begins in the village, not initially towards the burial cairn, but northwards, taking the road down the hill, with its beautiful views to the west over the Conway Valley to Moel Siabod. Soon woods encroach on both sides, climbing steeply up the hillside to the right and straggling along beside a shallow stream on the left. At the last house, called Bod Hyfryd, a very narrow lane is taken which climbs up the hillside beside the old woodland. It then drops into a narrow valley before rising again up to the farm of Gwninger. Beyond the farm, the lane becomes a track, with high banks lined with oak and ash and hawthorn.

As it climbs higher the view behind broadens out to cover all of the Carnedd Range, from the Ogwen Valley over the high tops of the main ridge to where it drops away towards the north coast. In early spring, the great east-facing cwms are rimmed with the last of the winter's snow, and the crags stand out, black and sombre above their hidden lakes.

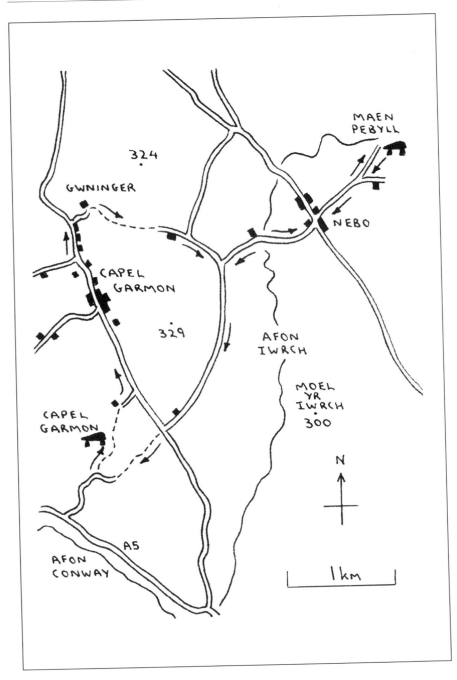

As the track levels out the trees are replaced by dense thickets of gorse, and it passes a derelict farm building before dropping gently down the eastern slopes towards the next valley. Ahead, the domed top of Moel Seisiog rises above the distant moors. The track once more becomes a lane, running through an area of beautiful, rolling, green fields and low hills flecked with sheep.

A left turn is taken and the road soon crosses the wide and shallow valley of the Afon Iwrch, 'the river of the deer' before climbing up again to the tiny village of Nebo. No more than a short street of houses on the edge of the moors, this tiny settlement boasts one of the finest views in Wales, with all the major mountain ranges of Snowdonia arrayed across the eastern horizon. A narrow lane leaves the village besides an old but still functioning water trough and climbs up towards the hills. After a left fork, the lane peters out near a small copse of pine trees and beside it lie the ruins of Maen Pebyll. This is the remains of a Neolithic long barrow.

Nowadays it sits in a quiet field at the edge of the moors, grazed by sheep and guarded by a friendly but ferocious-looking ram, but its name refers back to when it was a place of some significance. Maen Pebyll possibly means 'the meeting-place stone'.

Only three fallen uprights and a broken capstone have survived, but the shape of the original barrow can still just be made out. The capstone is beautiful, its pitted surface encrusted with lichens, ranging in colour from pinkish grey to the brightest of yellows, while dark green mosses erupt in tiny clumps from the many hollows and cracks on its sheltered eastern face.

I stood beside it one clear spring day and looked out towards the mountains. To the Moelwyns, away in the distant south-west, and to Moel Siabod with the Snowdon Horseshoe peering around its shoulders. To the Glyders, with the craggy summit of Tryfan just visible, and away to the long high ridge of the Carneddau fading away into a dark northern sky. It must have looked just the same four thousand years ago when the stones were dragged from the nearby moors and the great barrow was built.

From Maen Pebyll our route retraces its steps to Nebo, and back across the Afon Iwrch, to the road junction. Here, it turns away to the south and contours around the hill with the twin domes of the Arenigs rising in the distance ahead. At the next junction a stile leads up a mossy field to a beautiful viewpoint on a ridge between small rocky outcrops. It then drops down through a rather scruffy farmyard to a tiny lane, which is followed briefly, past the farm buildings to where another path turns back up the hill. This winds its way through scattered trees and rocky knolls to arrive at the famous long cairn of Capel Garmon.

Maen Pebyll burial chamber

Sitting among the small crags and natural rocks of the ridge in its own natural amphitheatre, the barrow is in a magnificent place. A chambered cairn of the Severn-Cotswold type it is very unusual this far north. It would originally have had two large circular chambers joined together with a long narrow chamber, all covered over with huge capstones. A low narrow entrance tunnel met the central area at right-angle while a larger false entrance was sited at the end of the cairn.

Nowadays the capstones have gone with the exception of one enormous slab covering the large circular chamber at the western end. Most of the uprights survive, with drystone walling between them and some interior stones possibly suggests a sub-division of the central chamber into smaller stalls. Most of the smaller cairn stones have gone but the shape has been reconstructed with a line of kerbstones.

The burial chambers would have been for the communal burial of the dead, used by the Neolithic people of the surrounding area. Most likely, selected bones of the ancestors would have been placed within them, to be taken out for special rituals or on significant days in the yearly cycle. It is thought that the open space created outside the false entrance could have been used for such events. The real entrance would probably have been small and hidden away in the side of the cairn.

The roofless entrance passage does, however, give us another clue as to why the tomb was sited where it was. It is aligned perfectly with a huge nat-

Capel Garmon

ural rock sitting on its own small hill just to the north. It has been suggested that this rock was a 'gorsedd' or natural throne, which would have been the original sacred meeting place, possibly for thousands of years before the cairn was built. Even then the great rock would have been a prominent feature, flat-topped and streaked with quartz veins and with all the great mountains of Wales arrayed before it.

It is amazing that the monument has survived as well as it has. In the past it was used as both a stable and a sheep-pen before it was partially restored and protected in the 1920's. The consequences of the restoration is that the cairn seems rather too neat and orderly to be the great age that it is, but at least it will not suffer the destruction that has befallen many similar sites.

From the barrow the path crosses the field, passing the great rock on its small hilltop to reach a lane, which takes you back to the road. From there it is but a short and pleasant walk back into the village of Capel Garmon.

This is a walk of two monuments set in a magical and time-worn landscape. One is largely destroyed and forgotten, the other restored and lovingly protected, and the contrast between them is great. However, both have managed to retain that magical 'sense of place' and each has its own special atmosphere that only develops through surviving over thousands of years of our history.

15. Carneddau Hengwm
Barmouth

Approx. distance: 8 miles

Approx. time: 5 hours

Starting point: Barmouth, GR 625165

Grade: A difficult walk over wild and remote moorland

O.S. Outdoor Leisure sheet: 18

Grid references: Cerrig Arthur, GR 632189; Bwlch y Rhiwgyr, GR 627201; cairn circle, GR 616204; Carneddau Hengwm, GR 613206

To the west of the high rocky spine of the Rhinog mountains is an area of wild and rugged moorland and scattered across it are many relics of our prehistoric ancestors. Standing stones and circles, burial chambers and cairns, many not marked on maps, lie largely forgotten and unvisited among a natural jumble of rocks and rough vegetation. Near the southern end of the range are the Carneddau Hengwm, two large and well pre-served-chambered long cairns which, but for their remoteness, would be as famous as many of our more treasured national monuments.

Our walk to them is not easy, and in low cloud or when the sea mists roll over the coastal ranges, good navigational skills are essential to find them among the confusion of old walls and natural boulders. But for all that, it is possibly their isolation that has saved them and adds so much to the atmo-sphere of the place, which stirs the imagination more than many a more famous site.

The route begins in Barmouth, but rather than walking from the centre it is best to drive up the steep side road to the car park by the Panorama Walk and begin from there. It initially follows the quiet lane northwards which climbs between rocky outcrops and through a natural woodland of sessile oaks. The trees are wonderfully twisted and intertwined, their trunks decorated with mosses, lichens, and even tiny feathery ferns hang-ing from the branches. These wild woods are the haunt of tree creepers and nuthatches and in the Summer months even the illusive pied flycatcher can occasionally be seen flitting from tree to tree in their dappled shade.

As the road climbs it breaks out into open pastureland with magnificent views up the Mawddach Estuary. At low tide the river twists and turns through reed-fringed sandbanks between wooded headlands dropping

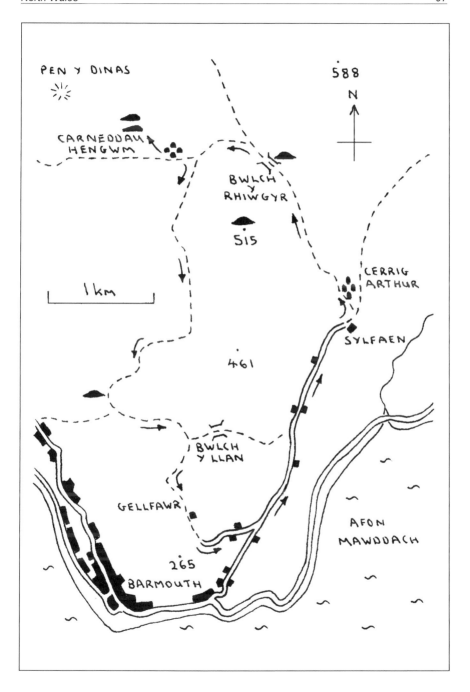

down from the hills. Beyond the wide valley, Cadair Idris rises in grand isolation, dominating the southern horizon.

The road ends at the farm of Sylfaen, and just beyond it a grassy farm track branches off to the left and climbs up and over a low ridge to where the strange remains of the Cerrig Arthur stone circle can be found on a small levelled terrace. This is a much-damaged site and as such is very difficult to interpret. Eight stones are still visible, forming a rough circle, although most have fallen and are partly grass-covered and two seem no more than large natural boulders possibly just rolled into place. Two more mounds in gaps in the circle could indicate stones now completely buried beneath the turf. In the centre of the ring, very unusually, are a group of three standing stones and some broken stone that look like the remains of a small burial chamber. If so, this is a great rarity in Wales, although examples of burial mounds within circles are more common in Scotland and the Lake District. It is also interesting that the circle is sited at the junction of two ancient tracks that lead up to the only crossable passes through the main spine of the Rhinog ridge to the coast.

The path continues across the hillside just below a wall built of huge blocks of stone. This is followed to the second gateway from where it is possible to turn and climb straight up to an upper wall. In places, this ancient track runs in a well worn channel, cut down below the level of the moor, indicating many centuries of use. In fact, a more recent track runs parallel to it in some places and is pleasanter underfoot. Above the top wall the moorland climbs quite steeply up to the pass, but any weariness is relieved by the views behind across the upper valley of the Afon Dwynant to where the great southern ridge of Diffwys sweeps up to its rocky summit.

The pass is narrow and well-defined, and the view westwards across Cardigan Bay is magnificent. At its crest are the remains of a large cairn. It is about thirteen paces across and bisected by a high wall, which was probably partly built with stones taken from the ancient mound. It is now no more than a raised ring on either side of the wall and should not be confused with the more visible modern cairn beside the path.

Beyond it the well-constructed track drops quite quickly down through a narrow, rocky defile to where the first wall on the left marks our route leading out across the lower slopes. This a strange area of wild moorland, enclosed by large well-preserved walls and our route crosses two 'fields' to an area of broken ground where the indistinct path forks. Taking the right fork it passes two strange, raised and intersecting rings of stones, before a gateway leads to an old settlement and the remains of a small Bronze Age kerbed cairn. The ruins of three small buildings and an embanked enclo-

Forecourt stones of Carneddau Hengwm

sure probably post-date the ancient cairn by several millennia but are a fascinating indication of the continuity of settlement on the moor.

At the far side of the same field are the chambered long cairns of Carneddau Hengwm. The first is a truly amazing structure, and is still largely intact, even after five thousand years of wild Welsh weather and human vandalism. It is a massive sixty-three paces long and twelve paces across running east to west. At its eastern end are three huge forecourt stones, which would once have blocked the passage into the burial chamber behind. This has, unfortunately, collapsed, but behind it the cairn rises and broadens over what could be another, still buried, chamber. Behind that a third chamber is amazingly undamaged and can still be entered through a narrow side passage. The small, low, circular space is surprisingly clean and dry, protected by its great capstone and retaining walls.

I remember sitting beneath its low roof, sheltered from the cold February winds that were scything across the moorland outside, and feeling such a powerful and enveloping sense of place and of timelessness. It was as if the thick and impenetrable fog of time was briefly swirling and thinning and opening around me. Few places I have visited have left me with such a strong feeling of belonging and being a part of a landscape and a continuing heritage.

The intact chamber of Carneddau Hengwm

The second long cairn, just to the north, is smaller and more damaged but its remaining capstone is a massive rectangular stone over four paces long and must weigh many tons. A drystone wall runs past the smaller barrow but rather inexplicably climbs over the larger one separating its first chamber from the rest, but even this fails to detract from the splendour of the situation. Looking westward from the cairns, the magnificent Iron Age fort of Pen y Dinas rises on its hilltop, and beyond it the coast runs northwards to Shell Island with the hills of the Lleyn Peninsula on the distant horizon. To the north, beyond the seemingly endless moors, the great dome of Moelfre stands isolated from the main ridge of the Rhinogs.

The route back is complicated and wild, but worth the effort. After retracing your steps to the fork in the path, the narrow track off to the right is taken and for almost three miles it picks its way across the westerly slopes of the main ridge. Initially it takes a level course following a long line of old manganese mine workings, before crossing them over a small but beautiful stone bridge and dropping down to the flat farmland below the moor. Passing the remains of an ancient cairn on the right, a good track then climbs back up almost to the pass of Bwlch y Llan, before dropping once more down along a green lane to the remote farmhouse of Gellfawr.

It is a marvellously wild area of jumbled rocks, in places piled in great confused heaps, overgrown with heather and gorse, and interspersed with damp reedbeds and patches of sphagnum moss. Through it all, the path is rarely obvious but navigation is helped by the stiles which are all in place and act as an invaluable guide. When in doubt, head for the next stile!

From Gellfawr a narrow lane leads pleasantly down, past the rocks of Barmouth Slabs with their far-reaching views across the mouth of the Mawddach, and back to the car park and the end of the walk.

This is a walk in wild and rugged country, and one which sums up the real essence of this book, for it visits a spectacular ancient monument, set in a dramatic and little changed landscape. It offers a chance to experience history relatively untarnished by the recent past, and as such is not to be missed.

16. Moelfre
Dyffryn Ardudwy

Approx. distance: 10 miles

Approx. time: 4 hours 30 mins

Starting point: Dyffryn Ardudwy, GR 587233

Grade: A long walk over wild and remote moorland

Outdoor Leisure sheet: 18

Grid references: Dyffryn burial chambers, GR 588228; Cors y Gedol burial chamber, GR 603227; standing stones, GR 637234 and, GR 627236; Bron-y-foel burial chamber, GR 607246

The sacred mountain of Moelfre rises dome-like over the wild and desolate moorlands to the west of the main ridge of the Rhinogs. Through this moorland, the Afon Ysgethin snakes its way down from the high rocky cwms to meet the sea near the village of Tal y bont. Scattered across this landscape are many megalithic sites, all that now remain to tell us about the Neolithic people who once lived and farmed on these on these quiet and peaceful fells.

Our walk begins in Dyffryn Ardudwy, a large village straddling the main road along the narrow coastal plain. The first, most well-known and most frequently visited of the sites is only a short walk from its centre. A signposted footpath down beside the small school leads you quickly and rather unexpectedly to the remains of the great, chambered burial cairn of Dyffryn.

This much-restored and well-cared for site sits in its own walled enclosure, close to buildings but sufficiently hidden from them to give some sense of seclusion. Two dolmens or burial chambers stand about ten paces apart within what is left of a huge cairn of large rounded stones over forty-five paces long and twenty wide. The smaller chamber is probably the older and originally sat within its own small cairn, which was later incorporated into the present cairn when the second chamber was added. Both the capstones are beautiful and although the larger one is now partly supported by brick pillars they make an interesting and contrasting pair. One can only imagine how the great cairn of white rock must once have looked standing as it did just above the breaking waves of the ancient coastline.

The path continues through an area of oak woodland and across a field to reach a quiet road climbing straight up the hillside. This rather monoto-

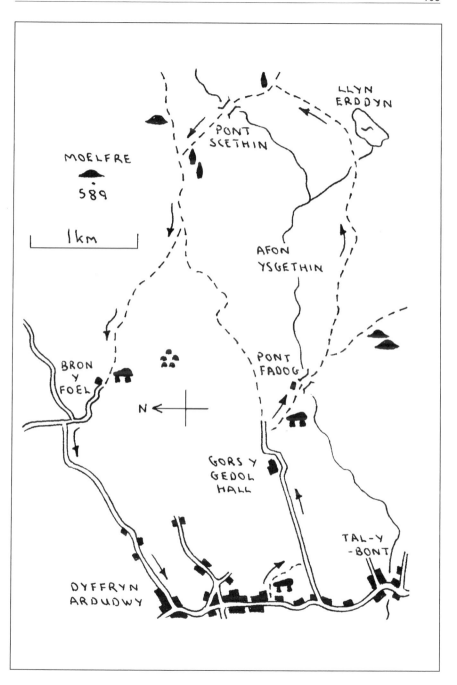

nous section of the walk is partly enlivened by the abundant wild flowers, which carpet the shade beneath the oak and lime trees that line the route. Eventually the lane skirts around the grand hall of Cors y Gedol and breaks out into a much more open and rugged landscape.

A rough lane branches off to the right and enters an area of jumbled rocks and gorse with a thin scattering of bent and twisted hawthorn trees. Another burial chamber sits close beside the lane looking, at first, little different from the natural scatter of rocks all around. Closer inspection, however, reveals a most beautiful dolmen supported at one end by only one large stone. I initially assumed that it had partly collapsed but there seems to be little evidence for other fallen support stones.

Perhaps it was built like this: there is certainly lots of room between the capstone and the hollowed-out floor. There is also evidence that the sides were walled up with smaller stones. The remains of a long barrow of rounded stones runs east to west and is over thirty paces in length.

It is not a spectacular site like Dyffryn, but it has everything that its more famous neighbour does not. Its moss-encrusted rocks seem to have been accepted into the natural landscape and merged with it. One stone in particular, standing beside the supporting stone, is marbled with a wonderful jigsaw pattern of different coloured lichens.

The sea is just visible in the col between low hills to the west and it is a wonderful place to sit and conjure up images of the people who raised the great stone and the ones who lay beneath it. Did they live nearby and raise sheep on the hills or did they live down by the coast and make ceremonial journeys up to the tomb where their ancestors were buried? I like to think that it was a part of their everyday lives and that the dead continued to be of importance long after they had gone. I think they would have felt pleased that the stone still stands and that people still visit it.

Beyond the barrow the lane dips gently down to the river which runs in a narrow and wooded valley, and is crossed by the beautiful Pont Fadog. Once across the bridge the lane peters out into a farm track, and after passing a short line of isolated Scot's pine trees enters the bleak and open moorlands.

It is a strange landscape of rocks and gorse and old stone walls. Birds are everywhere. Wheatears and pipits flit between the rocks, skylarks hang in the air and redstarts bow and flick their tails among the mossy stones.

Large piles of enormous boulders line the track as far as the eye can see, cleared from the still rocky hillsides for some unknown purpose. As the moorland levels out, the gorse bushes shrink to sheep-nibbled domes and reedbeds spread between the rocks. Above it all the great brooding dome of Moelfre dominates the northern horizon.

Before long the track crosses a stream, spanned by a single stone, and

Dyffryn Ardudwy

passes below Llyn Erddyn, which is close but hidden behind the low ridge to the right of the path. It is in a lovely wild spot and well worth the short detour to visit it.

Beyond the lake the track narrows to a path, in places paved with flat slabs, and crosses a level and almost featureless landscape. It eventually meets an old pony track dropping down from the high ridge of the Rhinogs, and the junction is marked by a standing stone. This small, black obelisk has white veins running through it and a scattering of old inscriptions etched into its shiny surface. From the stone, the often paved track turns down towards the river and the beautiful old bridge at Pont Scethin.

As it climbs up the slopes beyond and meets a gravelled lane, the first of two more small standing stones appears to the left of the path. The second one is just visible about a hundred metres away to the south-west. Neither stone is particularly striking and their purpose unclear, although they do align perfectly with the distant summit of Y Llethr, the highest point of the Rhinog ridge!

On my last visit to these stones the sea mists rolled in from the sea blanketing the moors and, search as I might, the ancient cairn marked nearby on the maps proved completely illusive. What I did discover, however, was hundreds of perfect, funnel-like spiders' webs in the heather. They appeared, as if by magic as the mists enveloped them and tiny jewels of water lit them up.

Bron-y-foel burial chamber

The track is followed downhill and across a stream to where a path branches off to the right. This traverses below an old walled settlement and drops gradually down across the moors. It soon becomes a green lane passing through a lovely area of small wide-walled fields and ruined cottages. Above, the high summit ridge of Moelfre miraculously appeared through a tear in the mists, as if suspended in the sky and disconnected from the land on which I walked.

As the first farmhouse comes into view, another burial chamber can be found built into a wall beside the lane. Again, like the one at Gors y Gedol, its great tilted capstone is only supported by one upright, and the chamber beneath enclosed with smaller stones. If this is how it was originally constructed, and all the obvious evidence suggests that it was, then perhaps it was a variation unique to this area. Whether intended or not, it creates a striking impression with the capstone pointing dramatically upwards. The remains of a small barrow can still be seen running into the field behind.

The lane continues past the farm between enormous walls to reach a quiet road, which winds pleasantly back through green and tranquil farmland to Dyffryn Ardudwy.

This is a walk of contrasts, of fertile fields and bleak moors, of sites restored and pristine, and others reverting to the natural landscape around them. All the way Moelfre can be seen high above the moors through the clearing mists, and away to the west the sea glistens in the late afternoon sunlight.

17. Moel Goedog Harlech

Approx. distance: 7 miles

Approx. time: 4 hours

Starting point: Harlech, GR 582310

Grade: Mostly straightforward walking along remote lanes, but with some steep hills and rather indistinct paths

O.S. Outdoor Leisure sheet: 18

Grid references: stone circle, GR 614312; cairn circles, GR 610324; Moel Goedog, GR 613325; standing stones, GR 609323, GR 608322, GR 607321, GR 604316, GR 602314 and GR 599309

This walk starts right in the centre of the old town of Harlech, but within twenty minutes it leads you into a remote and magical landscape almost completely removed from the 21st century. On the plateau above the narrow coastal plain, rocky hills rise above high sheep pasture and in the distance the black peaks of the Rhinogs ring the eastern horizon. Across this ancient landscape runs a prehistoric trackway marked by a line of standing stones. It leads towards the high hilltop of Moel Goedog and probably on towards the distant circle and cairn of Bryn Cader Faner some four miles further to the north-east.

The route begins by taking the steep hill road straight out of town before winding around several sharp bends to where a lane turns off to the left. This is followed to the cottage of Groes Lwyd with its wonderful views out across the sea. A stile beside the house gives access to the hill behind which can be climbed via a walled track past a ruined cottage to the large stone which marks its top.

What a place to sit! Snowdon and Moel Hebog rise up to the north and to the east the black sharp-edged ridge of the Rhinogs climb to the high, central peaks before dropping gradually down to the south. To the west, beyond the shimmering waters of Tremadog Bay, the rocky-spined Lleyn Peninsula dips away into the western sea. Closer at hand is the high farmland below, criss-crossed by wonderful stone walls and dotted with sheep. Above it rise sharp hills crowned with crags and scattered with rocks.

The path drops down to a quiet and remote lane and turning left along it you will quickly come to the first of the many standing stones which mark

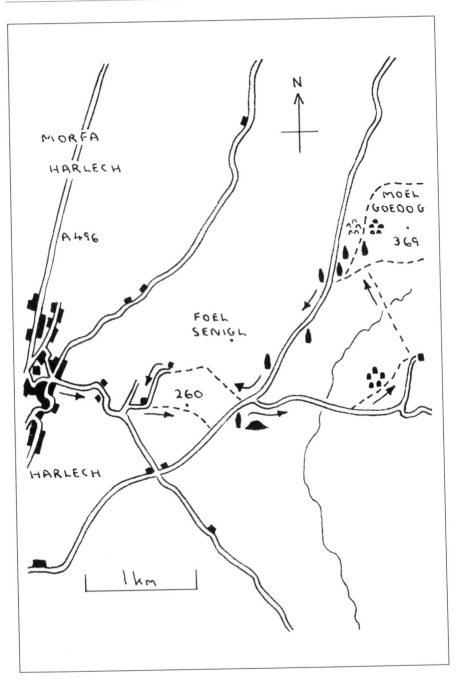

A tiny stone circle in the wild Rhinogs

the line of the ancient trackway. It is a beautifully shaped and pointed stone and stands almost six feet tall.

As I sat sketching it, buzzards circled high overhead and ravens croaked mournfully away on the rocks of nearby Foel Senigl. A hare loped across the field towards me, until sensing my presence it stopped before slowly turning away towards a dense thicket of gorse. Skylarks hung melodically in the air and a male wheatear swept low and silent along the line of the fence. Other than the sounds of the birds and the slowly drifting clouds, all was peaceful and still.

Just beyond the stone an even narrower gated lane turns off to the right and this drops down into a shallow valley through which runs a small stream. As it climbs up beyond it, several indistinct tracks turn off up the hill to the left. Between these paths, hidden away amongst the rocky out-crops of the ridge is a tiny stone circle.

Only three paces across, the six small stones sit on a levelled terrace looking out towards the highest peaks of the Rhinogs. The stones of the circle are of a slatey rock, and several have split and some are missing com-pletely, but nothing could detract from the magnificence of its position. I wonder why, some four thousand years ago, our ancestors decided to erect their tiny ring of stones in such a remote and lonely spot. Perhaps they lived nearby, possibly just down the hill where a small white stone cottage still sits in its own valley, hidden away from the modern world.

From beside this cottage a path climbs back up and over the rocky ridge and crosses a wide shallow valley to reach a track which circles around the now prominent hill of Moel Goedog. This leads back towards the lane and the line of the ancient trackway.

Just before the road is reached another track turns off to the right and climbs up onto the shoulder of the hill. Standing stones line the route now. Two stand near its junction with the road and two more are passed as you follow the track across the fields. Several others lying in the grass could well be stones that have now fallen.

Beyond the last stone the track levels out and, as it begins to drop away, two small rings of stones appear. One is above the track beyond the fence and is the remains of a kerbed cairn. About five paces across, the ring of low rough stones would once have held in the much smaller stones of a round burial cairn which have all but disappeared. The lower one is also small, but much more interesting and appears to be a ring cairn with an inner kerb of upright stones almost like a stone circle, surrounding a central levelled platform.

It may well have been similar to a larger one near Llyn Brenig, which has been partially restored. This also had a wide ring of stones whose inner edge was marked by small uprights surrounding an open space. When excavated, cremation burials were found within it, and a large post-hole at the very centre in which may once have stood a tall wooden pole. Perhaps this tiny ring was also built around a great carved totem pole and the cremated ashes of the dead lovingly buried beneath it.

Did the old stone-lined track lead to this ring of stones? Did it climb on up to the top of the hill, which is still ringed with the banks and ditches of an ancient settlement, or did it continue as the modern track does towards the great circle at Bryn Cader Faner. Certainly the stones stop here and so does our walk, for it now turns back and returns through the avenue of stones to the road.

Following the lane back towards Harlech is a pleasure. More standing stones appear, a small one to the left where the road seems to deviate from the original line of the trackway, and there may be others partly hidden within the enormous wide walls which line the route. As the road passes the rocky hill called Foel Senigl, a real giant appears just behind a wall. Over eight feet tall this great blade of rock is aligned along the line of the avenue. It is unlikely to be a coincidence that the tallest stone was sited at this, the highest point of the ancient track.

This one would have been visible for miles and adds weight to the theory that these stones were simple waymarkers. Many of the others, however, are small and so close together that a more symbolic purpose seems more likely. There is also some evidence to suggest that the stones were

One of the avenue stones below Moel Goedog

originally in pairs possibly forming a smaller version of the great ceremonial stone avenues of Avebury.

Beyond this huge stone the road drops back down to the first stone visited on the walk. Opposite it a path crosses a field, winding between gorse bushes and crossing a tiny stream before coming to a natural line of broken cliffs. Here small walled enclosures have been constructed at some time in the past, which abut against the crags. Several small huts or animal shelters still survive built entirely of stone and roofed with large stone slabs. One is roofed by a great tilted capstone, which must have slipped from the cliffs above.

The path then climbs through a small gate in a high wall and drops down a rocky field towards the obvious white cottage below. From there a track skirts around the hillside with beautiful views out to sea to reach the point where our route turned off up the hill at the beginning of the walk. The busy centre of Harlech is only a quick ten minutes away down the quiet lane.

This is an excellent walk. It passes through a magical and ancient landscape. Go when the sun shines for the views are breathtaking. Go in springtime when the birds are singing and go alone, for the tranquillity will overwhelm you. If you do, you will discover a land away from the rush of the modern world and one where it seems almost possible to revisit a time and a place when peace and solitude were not as rare as they have become today.

18. Ystumcegid Criccieth

Approx. distance: 4 miles

Approx. time: 2 hours 30 mins

Starting point: Rhoslan, GR 482408

Grade: A short but tricky walk along poorly marked footpaths

O.S. Explorer sheet: 13, or 254 in the new series

Grid references: Ystumcegid burial chamber, GR 498413; Rhoslan burial chamber, GR 484408

Although only short in length, the Afon Dwyfor drains the high cwms of Moel Hebog and the Nantle Ridge. In the winter months the melting snows make its water leap and tumble down the narrow Pennant Valley and along its short course to the sea. Below the mountains it loops around the low hills of Ystumcegid, 'the bend of the river where the hemlock grows', and above its rushing waters stands a remote and beautiful Neolithic burial chamber.

To reach it from the road is no great distance but it is a walk which requires a certain degree of determination, for the paths are not always obvious. It is, however, this feeling of remoteness that creates the unique atmosphere that is Ystumcegid. Standing in wonderful isolation on the slopes of a natural rocky tor, it looks out over the hills and valleys of the Lleyn Peninsula to the distant sea.

It starts in Rhoslan a small village on the road inland from Criccieth. Initially it follows the road northwards for a short distance until a narrow lane branches off to the right. This rises up a low hill between stone-banked hedgerows of gorse and hawthorn entangled with brambles, bracken and ivy. The fields to either side are rough pasture with scattered boulders and reedbeds and clumps of gorse. Ahead rise the mountains, the rugged ridges that ring Cwm Pennant and rise up to the smooth dome of Moel Hebog, 'the hill of the falcon'.

Beyond the hilltop, which is marked by a trig point in a wall, the lane drops into the valley of the Dwyfor, which here runs through a wild area of stunted birch and alder. Turning off the lane, a farm track soon leads to a pretty metal footbridge over the river, which flows crystal clear over deep rocky pools and weedy shallows. The dark shapes of fish dart in the shadows and herons stalk stiff-legged along the banks.

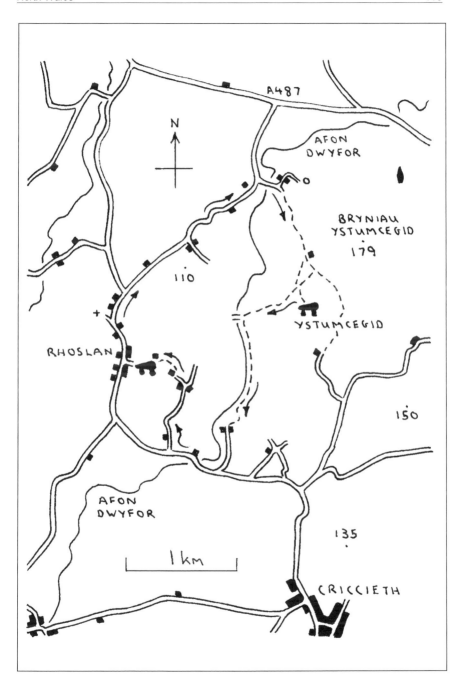

Once on the far bank the track leads up to the farm where paths turn off to the right and left. Our route takes the one to the right out onto rough grazing land, which is littered with huge rocks and dense thickets of stubby hawthorn and hazel bushes. Away to the left, beyond an old barn, are the remains of a hut circle, evidence that this area was settled well into the historic period. The track continues, crossing a shallow stream over a line of stepping stones and past a strange overhanging rock outcrop to reach a wonderfully wild wood. The old oaks are gnarled and twisted and the branches festooned with tiny ferns. Creepers twist around the trunks and everything is softly covered in mosses and lichen.

As the track leaves the wood it passes through the remote and abandoned farm of Ystumcegid-ganol. At the next gate the balanced capstone of the burial chamber comes into view on the crest of a low ridge dead ahead. The land between is marshy and difficult to cross, so it is better to take the track leading down to the right to another area of woodland where a rising path climbs up onto a rocky hilltop. Just beyond it, over a stile partially concealed behind a hawthorn tree, is the great tomb of Ystumcegid.

Standing in a field wall, the huge slab of the capstone is supported by four uprights, which raise it nearly five feet above the floor of its chamber. Triangular in shape, and surprisingly slender, it has been likened to a giant piano lid. The supporting stones are also quite delicate, giving the monument a look of fragility, which is only belied by its great age. One of the supports has a small stone wedged on top of it to allow it to reach the capstone and another only just touches it. A fifth upright serves to help enclose the chamber but takes no part in holding up the great roof. How it has remained in place for so long is a complete mystery!

Nothing remains of the cairn, although it was said to be of the Severn-Cotswold type, and the field wall probably contains most of the missing material. Several large stones still stand within the wall and may well be in their original positions.

It is very easy to clamber up onto the level capstone, and if one can ignore the precarious balancing act beneath, it is a perfect place to sit and admire the magnificent view. It is interesting to note that the nearby rocky hilltop has a scattering of huge boulders, which seem much chunkier and of a different rock to those which were used for the burial chamber. It is quite likely that this hill was the original sacred site. The large rocks, including one giant split stone, would have made this a place of some significance in ancient times, and like many other natural sites would have been the reason for the later choice of this hill for the burial chamber.

To return to the path it is necessary to go back through the boulder field and drop down to rejoin it by the woodland. The path then crosses a field

Ystumcegid

and becomes a good track leading down to the river and the footbridge. This is in need of some repair and should not be used. Instead follow the banks of the river southwards. This is a quiet and peaceful section of the walk and even a line of monstrous pylons crossing the river fails to spoil it.

The river flows quickly, tumbling over several small falls and rapids in a shallow valley. A tangled wood to the left spills down towards the path which winds along beside the waters edge. Only the sound of the water breaks the silence other than the buzzards which circle effortlessly above the trees. Eventually the path joins a farm track which leads past a large rock shaped like a pulpit leaning over the river, and through a campsite to a small lane. This returns to the river, which now runs through a deep wooded dell, and follows it to the road.

This is taken for a short distance, over an old stone bridge to where a narrow lane turns off to the right. This wanders through open farmland to the farm of Cefn-isa from where a driveway continues to an isolated bunga-low among the fields. A path then crosses a large field towards another secluded cottage and a through a gate leading back to Rhoslan.

In this last field, beside a small stream, is another burial chamber. Despite its proximity to Ystumcegid, the construction of this one is very different. A huge domed capstone weighing many tons rests upon four

Rhoslan burial chamber

remaining uprights. One complete side is open and unsupported, making it look rather like a megalithic bus shelter. Unusually, the back of the chamber is formed by a single horizontal slab running the entire length of the capstone. Of the three other supports one appears to have broken completely across but has remained in place because of the weight of the roof bearing down on it.

Again, nothing of the covering cairn remains, and this time it is difficult to blame surrounding field walls for being responsible for its destruction and removal. It has been suggested that many of the dolmen of Wales were intentionally exposed, perhaps thousands of years after they were built, as part of a later cult which still held the great stone tables in awe. It is certainly noticeable that many, like this one, retain no trace whatsoever of their cairn while others such as the Carneddau Hengwm remain virtually intact. Perhaps, as now, it was the stones which had became significant rather than the people who were buried within them.

Whatever the reason for its exposure, the result is a dramatic monument, the capstone in particular being a beautiful stone. Its top is covered in a blue-grey lichen with patches of deep green moss in its hollows. One of the uprights has several old initials scratched into it, one by an S.W.J. and dated 1813, which for some inexplicable reason seems to make it more acceptable.

From the burial chamber it is only a short walk, following the tiny stream, to a lane, which leads back into Rhoslan.

This is not an easy walk. The footpaths are often not marked, and although the stiles are all in place, following them can require some navigational skills. Having said that, they will take you, in what is essentially a farming landscape, well off the beaten track, and allow you to visit an ancient site that few others ever reach. Ystumcegid has no signposts pointing to it, it is not protected by fences and railings and no information boards will show you how it used to look. Go and find it on its rocky ridge and enjoy it for what it is, a piece of our history as unspoilt as it is possible to be.

19. Clynnog Fawr
Lleyn Peninsula

Approx. distance: 7 miles

Approx. time: 4 hours

Starting point: Clynnog Fawr, GR 415496

Grade: A straightforward walk along quiet lanes and little-used footpaths

O.S. Explorer sheet: 13, or 254 in the new series

Grid references: Holy well, GR 414495; Pennarth burial chamber, GR 430511; Clynnog Fawr burial chamber, GR 407495

The thin coastal strip of the Lleyn Peninsula to the south of Caernarfon, is dominated by the shapely cone of Gyrn Goch, 'the red-topped mountain'. Although not as high as the hills behind it, its dramatic shape and prominent position give it a significance beyond its height. This must also have been true in olden times, because huddled at its feet is the ancient settlement of Clynnog Fawr.

This was the site of one of the early Celtic monasteries, and the present fine Tudor church is said to be built on top of a much older megalithic monument. Just outside the village, in a field above a long pebbly beach, lies the small but beautiful dolmen of Clynnog Fawr. It is no coincidence that all these were sited directly beneath Gyrn Goch and beside a holy well whose water still springs from the sacred mountain behind. There can be little doubt that its importance as a religious site dates back well beyond Christian times to the shadowy era of our pagan past.

Even from the earliest of times the great, breast-shaped mother mountain of Gyrn Goch would have been revered and held in awe. The water which flowed from it would have been sacred too, thought to possess properties of healing and good fortune. When the people turned to the raising of great megalithic structures, it was only natural that they would site them beneath the holy mountain. With the coming of Christianity the continuity held, and Celtic monastery and Christian church simply replaced the older symbols of Man's allegiance to the sacred landscape around them.

This walk begins in Clynnog Fawr itself, and it is possible to explore the village before setting off. Better still, leave it to the end and climb up into the hills first. This gives you the opportunity to see the ancient settlement in its correct context as an integral part of the surrounding landscape.

From beside the small post office, a lane climbs steeply up, quickly leav-

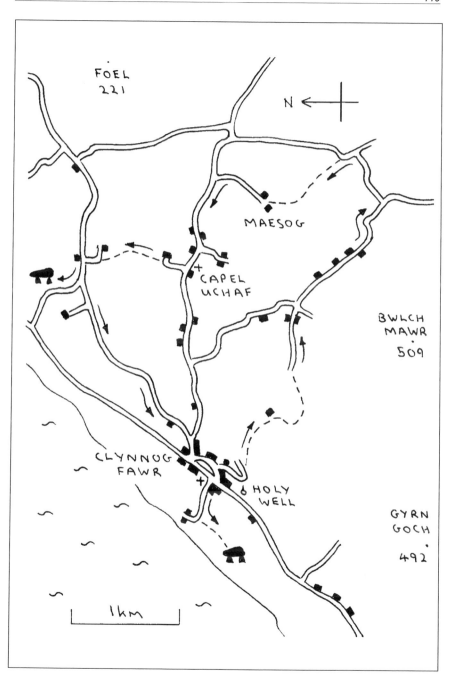

ing the narrow coastal plain behind until, after a sharp bend, a farm track branches off to the right. This rises between banks of ferns and gorse to where it opens out into farmland. Behind, the view expands with every step taken. The village is below and the sea beyond, with the west coast of Anglesey fading away towards a distant Holyhead mountain. To the left are low hills, one behind another, and straight ahead are the steepening slopes of the rocky-topped Bwlch Mawr.

The track continues, becoming a cobbled lane which runs right through the farmyard of Hafod-y-wern and out onto the open grazing land beyond. This is a semi-wild area of ferns and gorse and scattered rocky outcrops. In summer it is grazed by a large herd of cattle with many calves and a large but seemingly docile bull, which just turned and stared at me and my rather nervous daughter when we last passed.

This track soon becomes a narrow metalled lane running between stone walls, which are decorated with a fine array of wild plants. Ferns and purple heather sprout between the stones and heavily berried bilberries and blackberries grow along its top. Foxgloves and harebells add to the colour scheme that would not be out of place in a planted garden. Overhead, swallows and swifts wheel and glide and flocks of finches work their way along the lines of scattered hawthorn and rowan trees.

The abundance of wildlife is confirmed when you arrive at a small nature reserve. This is an area of meadow, wetland and scrub and is probably very similar to the landscape as it would have been in Neolithic times before the onset of intense farming 'improved' so much of the land. A huge variety of rare and wonderful wild plants still survives here, including the beautiful greater butterfly orchid. What a rich and colourful landscape our ancestors must have lived in.

The lane continues over a wild streambed to a junction where a left turn takes you down the hillside. At a sharp bend in the road, a footpath leads away to the left, which is signposted for Clynnog Fawr and Pontllyfni. It rises gently to a wonderful view point, with Anglesey clear to the north and the rocky Nantle Ridge of Snowdonia to the east. It also becomes clear how the mountain behind gets its strange name of Bwlch Mawr, 'the high pass'. It has a double summit and between them there is a grassy col leading onto the high plateau beyond.

The path then drops down past an isolated farm building to the remote farm of Maesog. The farm track soon takes you to a lonely road that can be followed through the scattered settlement of Capel Uchaf to where another track turns off, opposite the chapel of the same name. This soon becomes a path dropping down a slope towards the coast. It skirts around an isolated house to reach a lane running down to yet another of the tangled network of roads which wind around these hills.

The collapsed chamber of Pennarth

A left and a right turn bring you to our first megalithic site, the burial chamber of Pennarth, sitting in a field beside the lane. The beautifully shaped mushroom-like capstone has fallen and now rests at a crazy angle between the three upright stones. One of these has tilted outwards and was probably responsible for the capstone tipping over. The result is a strange but fascinating relic of the original chamber. A small amount of the original cairn material still surrounds the stones, but again, like so many of these ancient burial mounds, it appears to have been intentionally exposed at some time.

The walk back to Clynnog Fawr follows the quiet, hedged lane which winds between tall ash and rowan trees. The hillside to the left is wild and overgrown with dense thickets of ferns and scattered woodland, while to the right, stone-walled fields sweep gently down towards the sea.

Once back in the village, beneath the tall spire of Gyrn Goch, it is well worth exploring the ancient churchyard and sampling the waters of the holy well before setting off along the short track to the climax of the walk. A pleasant lane leaves the main road between the church and a lovely row of old stone cottages and heads towards the coast. At a sharp turn, a path turns off left, running between banks of water-smoothed stones topped with gnarled and twisted hawthorns. Ahead, the dolmen can be clearly seen at the end of a long avenue of gorse bushes lining the path.

This burial chamber is still intact, its wedge-shaped capstone delicately balanced on four surprisingly slender uprights. Beneath it is a rectangular pit possibly floored with flat stones and around it are many small stones, which are all that have survived of the covering cairn. The capstone itself is

Clynnog Fawr burial chamber beneath Gyrn Goch

encrusted in moss and lichen and on its upper surface are dozens of shallow cupmarks. These small, circular, man-made hollows are found on many ancient stones throughout the country but no one really knows their true significance. Were they art or did they form part of a religious ceremony? Were they carved simply to be admired, or were they an act of commemoration carried out by the bereaved? Whatever their purpose, they confirm that these ancient tombs were not merely practical repositories for the communal dead, but places of great spiritual importance where they could be honoured and immortalised.

These stones at Clynnog Fawr have stood beside the sea beneath Gyrn Goch for almost five thousand years. Even stripped of their covering cairn and surrounded by rusty iron railings, they retain something of this ancient sense of significance. For this is undoubtedly a special place, a place where history seems to leap out of the dusty pages of the past and briefly touches the present day. It is a place to sit and imagine the people who so laboriously shaped and raised the great capstone, and to remember those that were laid beneath it.

20. Tal y Fan
Conwy

Approx. distance: 8 miles

Approx. time: 4 hours

Starting point: Henryd, GR 761745

Grade: Long walk over beautifully wild moorland and hills, along paths that are not always easy to follow

O.S. Outdoor Leisure sheet: 17

Grid references: Standing stone, GR 747749; Maen Penddu, GR 739736; Cerrig Pryffaid circle, GR 724713; Cae Coch standing stone, GR 735717; Fron-y-Cawr, GR 737717; Maen-y-Bardd, GR 740718; Caer Bach, GR 744730; Fynnon St Celynin, GR 751737

The sacred hill of Tal y Fan sits in wonderful isolation high in the wild and dramatic landscape above the Conwy Valley. It is much lower than the great peaks of the main Carneddau Ridge away to the south-west, but it rises from lonely moors and dominates the view for miles around. Because of this and the fact that it stands high above the stone axe factory of Craiglwyd probably accounts for its importance to the Neolithic people of the area. Whatever the reason, it is ringed with standing stones and circles and ancient burial cairns that still stand, largely forgotten and untouched, in this pristine landscape.

The walk begins near the tiny hamlet of Henryd on the lower slopes of the Conwy Valley. Just beyond the village is the woodland park of Parc Mawr, and from its car park it is but a short walk up onto lonely moorland above. It begins along the quiet lane past a terrace of cottages but soon turns off onto a steep track, which climbs up through the oak woods. It is lined with old mossy walls and by banks covered in celandines and dog violets in the springtime. The track rejoins the lane and after a right turn beside the old house of Tyn Lon it climbs up into the more open landscape above the valley.

To the left of the lane is a field of stone piles. Eight pyramids of enormous boulders tower over the grazing sheep. Away to the right on a low ridge, a lone standing stone can be seen perfectly positioned on the skyline amongst scattered pines. The lane ends beside an old ruined cottage, which

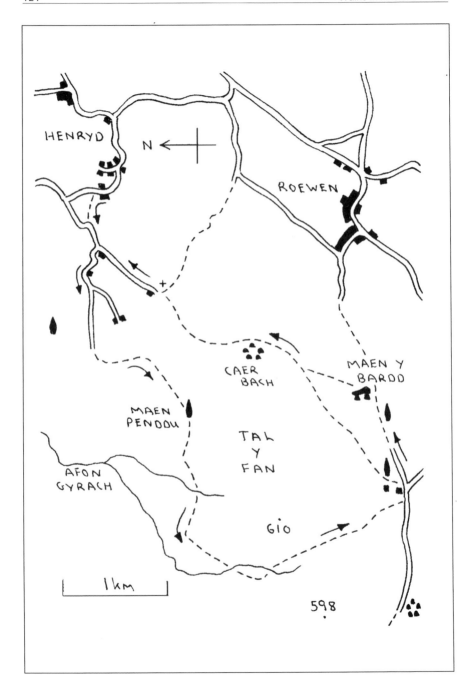

has magnificent views back towards Conwy Castle and the Great Orme beyond.

A farm track continues past a jumble of old stone sheep pens and out onto a moorland of gorse and scattered rock. After about a mile it arrives at the great menhir of Maen Penddu, 'the black-topped stone'. This huge standing stone marks the meeting of two ancient trackways from the Conwy Valley, which merge before continuing over the moors towards the Neolithic axe factory to the north. Beautifully smoothed and rounded, it rises almost like a ship's prow at the centre of a shallow basin between low hills.

Beyond the stone, the track continues for a short way until it turns uphill towards an old quarry. At this point a path branches off to the right skirting around the lower slopes of Tal y Fan. This is wonderful walking, the hill rising steeply to the left, and to the right a wide basin of wild and empty moorland sweeping away towards distant hills.

The whole area is a haven for wildlife. Small groups of wild horses graze amongst the scattered rocks and the patches of gorse and heather. These small, long-haired ponies roam freely over the northern Carneddau and seem largely unperturbed by the occasional passing walker. Birds seem to be everywhere. Stonechats balance precariously on the spiky gorse, wheatears and tiny pipits flit amongst the rocks and in the sky the song of the skylarks rises and falls on the wind.

Below the path can be seen a strange stone structure, a peat house, used for the drying and storing of peat from the moor in past centuries. Built of large blocks and roofed with large flat slabs, it seems almost megalithic in construction. It is in a magnificent spot, wild and desolate, surrounded by hills and moorland fading away in all directions.

Beyond the old house the track rises up and around the shoulder of Tal y Fan. Away to the right, the famous Druid's Circle can just be made out in the distance, between two low hills. As the indistinct path climbs into a high cwm, the landscape changes quite dramatically. The gorse and grass moorland is replaced by a dense cover of heather and the rattle of disturbed grouse takes the place of the more melodic song of the skylark. The path keeps to the left, just below the steeper slopes until it reaches the col marked by a wall and a stile.

From here it is possible to climb a short steep path up to the top of Tal y Fan, and the effort required is more than compensated by the magnificent view in all directions from the summit cairn. The high rolling ridge of the Carneddau runs away to the south, mountain rising beyond mountain, towards the great cairned top of Carnedd Llewelyn. To the north are

Maen-y-Bardd

Anglesey and Conwy Bay, and in the east, the low hills and moors of Denbighshire fade away into the distance.

The path down from the col is well-walked and signposted and brings you quickly to a quiet moorland road. The walk can be extended from this point by following it along to the west for about half a mile. Just beside the lane is a circle of tiny stones known as Cerrig Pryffaid, 'the perfect stones', which were presumably named before the rather intrusive electricity cables were erected uncomfortably near by!

Instead turn east and follow the lane for about a hundred metres until it turns down the slope towards the Conwy Valley. Our path continues straight on, along a lovely walled track. Marked on the maps as a Roman road, it is in fact much older than that. This is an ancient trackway, lined with huge blocks of stone, which runs from the pass of Bwlch y Ddeufaen down to an old crossing point of the River Conwy. Evidence of its prehistoric provenance soon appears to the left of the track. A large standing stone, shaped like a giant thumbnail, stands on a low rise in the field.

A little further on is another, this time on the right behind the high wall. Known as Ffon-y-Cawr, 'the giant's staff', this seven-foot pillar leans at a crazy angle to the south towards the distant hillfort of Pen-y-Gaer from where it was reputedly thrown! It can be visited by continuing for a short distance along the track to where a footpath crosses the field.

Caer Bach

Just beyond this is Maen-y-Bardd, 'the poet's stone'. This is a beautiful dolmen of four uprights supporting a wonderfully balanced capstone. Beneath this great stone is a small, almost circular burial chamber. Legend has it that anyone spending the night there would awake either mad or a poet! My ten minutes there did neither, but it did fill me with amazement that this wonderful and atmospheric monument has remained virtually intact for nearly five thousand years. The original covering cairn has largely gone, robbed for the many surrounding field walls, but this has at least exposed this most beautiful of structures for us all to appreciate.

It is a place to sit and imagine, to picture it as it was, to recreate in your mind the days of the raising of the great stone, of the internment of the honoured dead and of the ceremonies which would have taken place beside it. Were they quiet days of sadness and weeping, or were they days of celebration and music as another soul passed forever beyond the stones?

From the dolmen a faint track can be taken which climbs up and across the hillside through wonderfully windswept hawthorns to a high, unbroken wall running down the slope. This is crossed by old stone steps, which climb up and over it to a field leading up to an iron gate in the upper wall. Beyond the gate is a good level track running across the hillside.

This track leads you into a magical landscape of short turf, dotted with wonderfully sculptured domes of gorse. Large, naturally-smoothed rocks lie scattered across the rolling ground, and above, rocky pinnacles pierce the skyline. I watched a buzzard, perched on the highest of the huge blocks, rise and circle lazily overhead, wing tips spread against a blue and cloudless sky.

Before long this track passes just below Caer Bach, a small hill ringed with a shallow ditch and outer bank. Despite its name this was not a fort. It appears to be a type of henge, probably from the Bronze Age, for inside the ditch are the remains of a ring of stones running around the top of the hill. Much loose cairn material lies scattered around, and in the centre is one large stone block of almost white quartz. Whatever this site was, it is a fascinating place to explore, lonely and removed from all traces of the modern world.

Beyond Caer Bach, the track curls around a small subsidiary hill before dropping pleasantly down to farm buildings beside a beautiful 14th century church. This was built beside the even more ancient and sacred well of Ffynnon Celynin, again on the line of the prehistoric trackway down to the River Conwy. From the church a tiny lane can be followed easily back down to where the walk began.

21. Cefn Coch
Penmaenmawr

Approx. distance: 4 miles

Approx. time: 3 hours

Starting point: Penmaenmawr, GR 723763

Grade: A short but steep walk along well-marked paths and tracks

O.S. Outdoor leisure sheet: 17

Grid references: Bryn Derwydd stone circle, GR 732751; standing stone, GR 731749; Circle 275, GR 725748; Druid's Circle, GR 723747; Meini Hirion, GR 722747; ring cairn, GR 722746; stone circle, GR 719747; Cors y Carneddau cairns 717747; Craiglwyd axe factory, GR 717749

At the northern tip of Snowdonia the high ridges of the Carneddau plunge almost vertically into the Irish Sea. The old town of Penmaenmawr clings precariously to the steep slopes between the twin headlands of Penmaen Mawr and Penmaen Bach above where the main road and the railway run beside the coast. Rising above the town is Cefn Coch, the 'red ridge', a line of high hills heralding the start of a great sweep of moor and mountain running unbroken southwards for all of twelve miles, into the mountainous heart of Wales.

On the northern rim of this high plateau is an area of ancient settlement, centred around the Stone Age axe factory of Craiglwyd, which is as complex and well-preserved as anywhere in the country. From Craiglwyd, 'the grey crag', prehistoric trackways radiate outwards along the high ridges to the west and east and south, and beside these can be found a great range and diversity of ancient ceremonial sites and monuments.

This walk begins in Penmaenmawr, in the upper section of the town where the 'mountain lane' begins its climb up through stands of mature beech trees towards the high ridge above. It is a steep and tiring climb, fortunately partly relieved by the ever-expanding view behind out over the coast to Anglesey and the Great Orme. The metalled road comes to a sudden end, turning into a rough farm track as it crosses the steep lower slopes of Foel Lus.

The farmland ends now and the track climbs through an area of rough grassland mottled with patches of heather, gorse and bracken and a scattering of wind-battered hawthorn trees. At the first col the crowded and busy

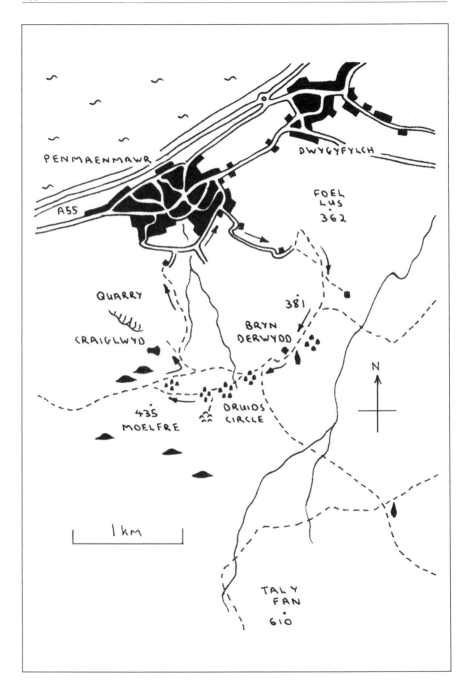

coast is left behind and ahead the wild moorland of the Carneddau rise towards the long rocky crest of Tal y Fan away to the south. Here the track splits, the left branch continuing to the isolated farmhouse of Tyn y Ffrith, while our route curls away to the right contouring around the lower slopes of Craig Hafodwen.

As the track approaches the last remote house of Bryn Derwydd, which is partly hidden within a copse of trees, the first of a line of stone circles can be seen in a field to the left. Only four small stones remain clearly visible, but from the gentle curve of the arc that they form, it would seem that the original circle was large – over twenty paces across.

Just beyond it, and standing close to the house is a huge standing stone, wider than it is high, and weighing many tons. Aligned with the ancient trackway, it was probably a marker stone, similar to those that line the ancient pathways near Moel Goedog in west Wales, and Maen Penddu standing at a crossroads of prehistoric tracks just a mile to the south.

The farm track ends at the house and becomes instead a pleasant path of wonderfully springy turf, which winds between perfectly sculptured mounds of gorse and many scattered rocks. Herds of wild ponies live on these hills and can often be seen standing out against the sky on a far ridge or even grazing leisurely beside the path. Sociable and unconcerned by passing walkers these small shaggy-haired animals grace the landscape and seem as much a part of it as the hoary stones they live amongst.

The path rises to a col between low hills. This is a marvellous place. The old track runs on towards Craiglwyd, the craggy ridge now visible ahead and the sea fills the northern horizon. To the left the land rises to an undulating crest crowned by the tall stones of the Druid's Circle. Standing close beside the path, often unnoticed and largely ignored, is another circle, tiny but all the more fascinating for its diminutive size.

Five low rounded boulders forms a ring barely three places across. Within the circle the ground was once covered with white quartz, which also filled a small pit in its centre. The heaviest of the stones, facing the south-west, is positioned on its side, a tiny recumbent stone. Unique in Wales, this type of five-stone circle is more usually found across the sea in southern Ireland. Most likely it was built in the early Bronze Age, at least a thousand years later than the larger circle on the skyline above.

This is reached by following a grassy path up the slope, and over two small streams to where it sits on a high, level platform. It is a large Neolithic circle of about twenty stones of varying size and shape, built into a low stone bank in an oval shape almost thirty paces across. Two stones in the south-west section are turned outwards to form an entrance. Some of the

A tiny five-stone circle below the Druid's Ring

stones are over six feet tall and several have shapes so distinctive that legends have grown up around them.

One, known as the Stone of Sacrifice, has a smoothed ledge on its outer face and is the only one to have another stone facing it outside the circle. Another, the Deity Stone, so closely resembles a hooded and sinister figure that it was thought to stand in judgement on anyone who stood before it. The legends almost certainly post-date the circle by thousands of years, although it is quite possible that their shape did in fact have some significance for the original builders.

What is known is that within the ring were several Bronze Age cremation burials of small children along with a number of grave goods interred beneath a low scatter of loose stones.

Less than a hundred metres further on are the remains of another ancient site, supposedly another circle, although this is now difficult to visualise. All that is left is a strange jumble of stones, some of which seem indeed to form a small low ring, while others stand in a straight line beside it, with others scattered seemingly at random. It is known as Meini Hirion, the 'tall stones', and it remains a mystery, but is all the more interesting for that.

From Meini Hirion a narrow path leaves the main track and turns inland for about fifty metres to where yet another site can be found. It is a ring cairn, a flat circular bank of small stones surrounding an open space about fifteen paces across. Several stones also lie in the centre and a number of larger ones stand within the outer ring. As with many of these ancient sites it probably evolved over the centuries, changing its form and use several times. Quite possibly it was a stone circle originally, and like the Druid's Circle, the circular bank was a later addition.

After returning to Meini Hirion, the path continues downhill to rejoin the lower track. Between the two paths the grassy slope is covered with a scattering of natural boulders. Another supposed stone circle close to where the paths meet seems little more than a curve of natural rocks, almost indistinguishable now from the surrounding boulder field.

More obvious is a large burial cairn beside the path several hundred metres further on. In fact, it is just one of a group known as the Cors y Carneddau cairns which lie on the col between the small dome-like hill of Moelfre and the ridge of Craiglwyd. The first and most intact is a huge mound of loose stone with a collapsed and hollow centre. This one is easily visited but, unfortunately, the others are beyond the high stone field wall to the right of the path. Less well preserved, these now consist of little more than rings of large kerb stones, their interiors probably taken when the wall was built.

Just beyond them is the site of the ancient axe factory, from where highly polished and prized blades were distributed widely over the country and even across the sea to the Isle of Man and Ireland. The significance of these axes is shown by the number which have been found unused and intentionally buried within many sacred sites.

Unfortunately no access is available from the col, and the route instead turns back along the lower path to where a signpost points the way downhill towards the coast. This good track crosses a shallow marshy stream over a long, low, raised walkway. From the far end it is possible to turn back uphill and climb steeply up, through a broken wall, to visit the rocky outcrops of Craiglwyd. Little remains, but it is interesting to see how the hard volcanic rock is black and almost glass-like where it has been broken. Mounds of loose chippings above the undercut crag are mostly grassed over but it is still possible to find chippings in places where the surface has been disturbed.

The path down from the raised causeway is steep at first, running beside the stream as it cuts down into a wild and wooded gorge. It then breaks off across the open hillside through an area of scattered ash and hawthorn trees. These are alive with flocks of pipits, redwings and fieldfares on cold winter days when the moors above seem almost devoid of life but for the occasional solitary raven high in the sky.

The Stone of Deity

The path eventually drops to a farmhouse and rejoins a lane running back into Penmaenmawr and the end of the walk.

Short, but packed with ancient sites, this walk shows how this area remained a place of some significance for thousands of years and was a focal point for trackways which spread out across Wales and beyond. Its importance was also known across the sea in Ireland, from where boats must have sailed to trade for the highly prized volcanic stone of these hills. Close to the larger circles built by the local people, they must have raised their own tiny ring as a place of worship, looking out over Craiglwyd and across the sea towards their distant homeland.

Anglesey

The portal stones of Bryn Celli Ddu

22. Bryn Celli Ddu
Llanfair Pwllgwyngyll

Approx. distance: 4 miles

Approx. time: 2 hours 30 mins

Starting point: Llanddaniel Fab, GR 496706

Grade: Short walk along quiet lanes, farm tracks and little-walked footpaths

O.S. Outdoor Leisure sheet: 17

O.S. Explorer sheet: 263

Grid references: Bryn Celli Ddu chambered cairn, GR 507702; Llanddaniel Fab standing stone, GR 503704; Bryn yr Hen Bobl chambered cairn, GR 519690; Plas Newydd burial chamber, GR 520697

Just over the Menai Straits is the quiet valley of the Afon Braint. Beside its shallow waters is one of the best preserved and most impressive of all the Neolithic monuments of Wales, the great, chambered cairn of Bryn Celli Ddu, 'the mound at the dark grove'. Several other important burial chambers lie quite close by. The ruined dolmen of Ty Newydd and the huge chambered longcairn of Bryn yr Hen Bobl can be found about a mile away to the east, within the grounds of the Plas Newydd estate.

Our walk begins in the village of Llanddaniel Fab and follows the lane running south-west from the crossroads at its centre. Just as the houses end a track turns off to the left and runs down into the shallow valley. As it turns towards the farmyard of Felin Rhosgering, a path continues across a rough field to a footbridge over the stream. Beyond the stream the path leads on to another farm and a lane. Once on the lane the first gate on the left allows you to follow an unmarked public footpath to a track running through the farm of Glanyrafon and on to the road. The route then turns back north along the road to where a signpost points to a path running along the banks of the river towards Bryn Celli Ddu.

This first section of the walk is rarely done and the footpath is unmarked in places and not always obvious. This same spot can be reached by simply following the road from Llanddaniel Fab south-east to where it crosses the stream, although this considerably shortens the walk.

Away to the right above the trees, the great peaks of Snowdonia ring the southern horizon. Carnedd Dafydd and Carnedd Llewelyn, dark and

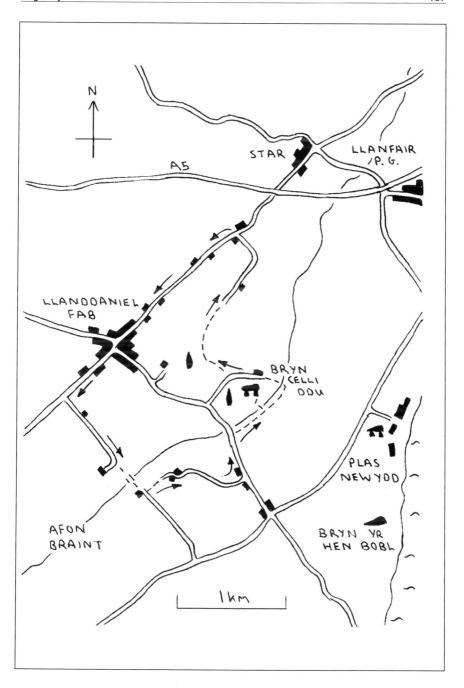

snow-streaked, rise above the lower ridges. Several rocky outcrops in the adjacent fields show that once this must have been a much wilder and rock-strewn landscape than the pleasant pastoral scene that the stream flows through now.

The path soon crosses a new wooden bridge over the stream and continues along the opposite bank before turning at the first wall towards the great burial cairn, which can be clearly seen in the next field.

This is a magnificent monument, although it has been partly reconstructed and no longer really looks like it would have done during any of the many phases of its history. The original structure was probably a henge, a circular area enclosed by a ditch and an outer bank, with a stone circle inside it. The remains of the ditch can still be clearly seen but the outer bank has all but gone. Several large stones within the boundary of the cairn could well be all that remains of the older free-standing circle.

At some later date, possibly many hundreds of years later, a burial chamber was constructed within the henge and a great cairn built over it. So large was the cairn that it overlapped the ditch and partly filled it in. What remains is a much-reduced cairn, only covering the chamber itself, the kerb of the larger mound and the remnant of the ditch from the original henge.

Ignore all this and enjoy it for what it is, an atmospheric and spectacular window into our past! As you squeeze between the portal stones and creep along the narrow entrance passage, the chamber beyond is streaked with shafts of light leaking in through a gap between two of the huge uprights and the largest of the capstones. At the end of the passage, the small hexagonal vault seems dark but the narrow rays of afternoon sun strike a dramatically placed and almost sinister column of black stone, free-standing within the chamber. This beautifully worked and smoothed pillar, tapering slightly at top and bottom, is almost human in shape and size and so frightened the first excavators that, apparently, they fled the tomb in panic! Whether it was placed for just such a purpose or not, this black sentinel stone had watched over the bones within the chamber for thousands of years. It is unlike any other worked stone I have ever seen.

Outside the cairn was another stone of great beauty. Carved on both sides it once stood buried deep within the centre of the original mound. This stone now sits rather sadly and incongruously in the National Museum in Cardiff, but a replica stands in its place. As the afternoon sun lowers and the shadows grow, the faint curves and spirals carefully etched into it, seem to suddenly spring to life and writhe, and twist and turn across its rough surface. For such a thing of beauty to be buried must have meant

The sentinel stone of Bryn Celli Ddu

that the carvings were of great symbolic importance, although the meaning behind the symbolism has died long ago with the people within the tomb.

From the top of the cairn it is possible to look out towards the mountains of Snowdonia to the south-east, but it is the view in the opposite direction which is even more fascinating. In the next field is a huge flat-topped rock outcrop, a 'gorsedd' or natural throne, an ancient and sacred site, probably worshipped at long before the henge was built beside it. In the same field is a small and isolated standing stone, but it is another, a much taller and dramatic one, which catches the eye. Llanddaniel Fab menhir, a slender blade of rock stands about five hundred metres away on a low hill, in perfect alignment with the top of the natural altar.

To continue the walk towards this distant stone it is necessary to retrace your steps back to the bridge over the river, and follow the far bank along to the next crossing point. A narrow bridge leads to a muddy field beside an

Llanddaniel Fab Menhir

old cowshed and over a stile to a lane running past the farmhouse of Bryn Celli Ddu. The road passes the natural outcrop and as it bends away behind it a path turns off to the right and follows a tiny clear stream running down towards the Afon Braint.

The standing stone rises majestically on the crest of a low hill in the middle of the next field, away from the path which skirts around to the right. It is a beautiful stone of grey schist, which has tiny facets of mica which shine in the sun. It is streaked with veins of white quartz and encrusted with grey and orange lichens. It is over ten feet high and seems even taller, and it stands amid a cairn of large stones. These may be the result of more recent field clearance although several do seem to have been placed purposely to support the standing stone that rests on the natural bedrock.

From the stone it is possible to look back towards the burial mound whose high dome is just visible over the flat crest of the outcrop. Even more fascinating is that, from this direction, the alignment continues, for directly above Bryn Celli Ddu is the summit of Carnedd Llewelyn. This dominant peak crowns the high ridge of the Carneddau range and is itself a sacred place. It has a line of large ancient cairns, visible even at this distance, running along its rocky skyline.

For four such significant sites to be lined up so perfectly must be more than mere coincidence, and if so, why were these alignments so important? Did they help the spirits of the ancestors to rise from their tomb towards the mountain top from where they could look over and protect their descendants? Did they stand at the stone and watch smoke from the pyres beside the chamber rise up over the natural throne towards the summit of the mountain? We may never know, but it is a place to let the imagination loose to drift back over the centuries to try to picture the scene.

The path itself skirts a damp, marshy area in the corner of the field, where, if you are lucky you might see snipe, which crouch in the tall reeds, and explode into flight as you pass. It crosses the next field to reach the end of a farm track, which passes through an old farmyard to a lane. This soon brings you back to the road which can be followed pleasantly back to the village, accompanied all the while by the magnificent views of Snowdonia away to the south-east.

This is a short walk but one which is full of interest. It presents us with many questions which we can no longer answer, and what remain are but a few pieces of a much larger and more complex puzzle. Perhaps it is what is missing as much as the few stones that survive which make this such a fascinating area to explore.

23. Tre Dryw Brynsiencyn

Approx. distance: 6 miles

Approx. time: 3 hours

Starting point: Brynsiencyn, GR 485671

Grade: An easy walk across fields and along quiet lanes

O.S. Explorer sheet: 263

Grid references: standing stones, GR 477677 and GR 475678; Bodowyr burial chamber, GR 462682; Tre Dryw stone circle, GR 462669; Castell Bryn-gwyn henge, GR 466671; Caer Leb, GR 473675; Brynsiencyn burial chamber, GR 480667

The Afon Braint, the most sacred river of Anglesey flows between low hills to join the Menai Straits as it opens out into the Irish Sea. Its wide and shallow valley is littered with standing stones, henges and circles, and burial cairns still stand on the rising slopes to either side. Just a few miles above where it spills out onto the sands of Traeth Abermenai once stood the great Neolithic ceremonial complex of Tre Dryw.

Today, the few tantalising clues that remain are just enough to allow us to reconstruct in our minds the magnificence of the scene thousands of years ago. Standing on low bluffs just above the marshy valley floor stood a small circle of enormous stones, surrounded by a wide bank and ditch. Several hundred metres away to the north-east, and probably linked originally by an avenue of stones, was a circular henge whose high stone bank was surrounded by an outer ditch. Between the two, it is thought there may once have stood a great cairn of white quartz stones, possibly giving rise to the name of Bryn Gwyn, 'the white hill', for the nearby farm.

To reach this ancient complex our walk begins in Brynsiencyn, and follows the main road westwards through the village until a track turns off to the right between the last of the houses. After about two hundred metres a footpath leads out onto open fields, which are crossed to reach a range of farm buildings. The well-marked path continues and in the second field two standing stones appear, one off to the right of the path and one directly ahead.

The first one is a very solid, square-cut stone about five feet high, and the second is of similar height but is a much more massive stone, over eight

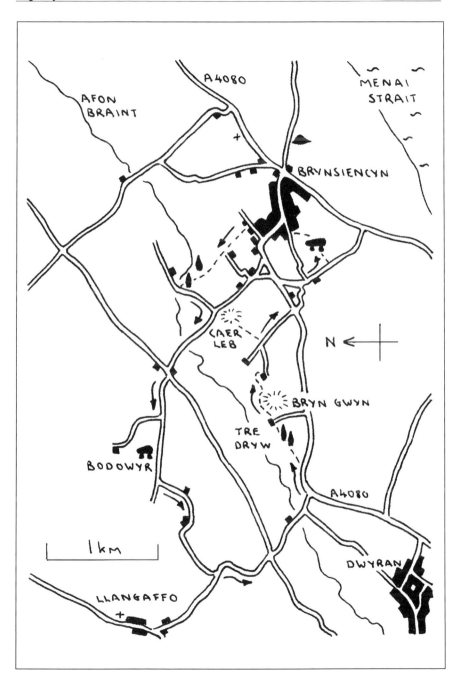

feet wide. Both stones have veins of quartz running through their wavy volcanic grain.

It is difficult to get any sense of their original purpose. They stand in isolation, separated from each other by a low rise in the ground. They both stand on the slopes above the Afon Braint, and are aligned with a nearby crossing point of the river, and also with the dolmen of Bodowyr on the hill beyond. Perhaps they were simple waymarkers leading the way through what would then have been a marshy and wild river valley towards the great cairn. The broad face of the second stone is certainly turned to allow it to be easily seen as the route is followed.

Instead of following along this direct line, our path turns down a farm track to the road, which drops down to a bridge over the river. The shallow stream meanders between banks of tall reeds and has probably changed little since the time our ancestors followed the same route. Beyond the river the lane climbs slowly, over a staggered crossroads towards Bodowyr.

On a fine spring day these lanes are a delight to walk along. Wildflowers grow in profusion along the verges and as the ground rises the great hills of Snowdonia appear away to the south-east. On the last occasion that I walked along them it was all very different. On a very wet day in August the clouds hung low and heavy over the trees. Only a few tired foxgloves and campions drooped over the already browning grasses, and the wild and tangled hedgerows glistened in the damp air.

Just off the lane to the right is the beautiful burial chamber of Bodowyr. Three uprights support a large mushroom-shaped capstone over what would once have been a circular chamber. A fourth upright blocks the end and a fifth has fallen outwards. All signs of the original covering mound have long gone.

Sitting within a field of tall wheat, and enclosed by the rain and mist, the sense of isolation was almost complete. As I sat sheltering from the rain beneath the capstone I noticed that its underside is decorated with a swirling pattern of quartz veins and tucked between it and one of the uprights some one had placed a small twist of wheat and wild flowers.

Even the name is interesting, Bodowyr, possibly means 'the house of Ur', who was the great Neolithic goddess of the Earth. Could the name really have lasted for as long as the stones have stood?

Beyond the burial chamber the lane continues, winding between high hedgerows, to the crest of a low hill. Away to the right the church spire of Llangaffo rises on a parallel ridge beyond a shallow tributary valley of the Braint. The tiny lane joins a road, which drops down to cross the river at the old bridge of Pont Mynach. Away to the left, beyond an immaculate garden, the valley bottom can be seen looking wild and uncultivated, probably very

Bodowyr

like it must have done thousands of years ago. Beyond the bridge our route rejoins the main road for just a short distance until a footpath leads out left on to the fields above the river.

Hidden at first in the high tangled hedge, it is not until you almost reach them that the great stones of Tre Dryw appear. These two giants are unequalled in Wales and compare in size only with those of Avebury or the great circles of the Scottish islands. The tallest is at least fifteen feet high, a wide blade of rough volcanic stone. The shorter one is itself over ten feet tall and is a massive monolith emblazoned with stripes of white and rose quartz and with a sloping top like the famous stones of Orkney. The two could not be more dissimilar and it is hard to imagine what the complete circle would have looked like.

Several hundred years ago, when they were first recorded, two other stones stood with them, forming an arc, and an outer bank and ditch could still be seen. Now only these two remain, but their size and the unexpectedness of their sudden appearance still takes the breath away. Even the old rusty gate between them and the ivy growing up the side of the larger one does not seem to detract from their splendour.

If you stand in the field beyond and look back, on a fine day the great chasm of the Llanberis Pass is framed in the distance between the stones. But on my last visit, the mountains were hidden in a veil of dark clouds and

The great stones of Tre Dryw

the mist hung low over the island. The stones looked black and sinister and ran with rain. In the relatively unsophisticated times of the past this must have been a truly awe-inspiring place.

The path continues past an isolated house, possibly the original site of the white cairn, to the henge of Castell Bryn Gwyn. A high circular bank encloses an area about fifty metres across. The northern section was destroyed when a farm was built into it and a track also eats into the eastern side. Originally the bank would have been of bare stone surrounded by a ditch, and would have been entered through the obvious causeway on the south-west side.

Excavations have shown that wooden structures once stood within the henge, although what they were is unclear. As well as Neolithic flints and pottery, other artefacts from the Bronze Age right through to the Roman period suggest it continued to be used in some way for thousands of years.

From the henge the path goes around the back of the farm, crosses fields to reach another house and a track leading back towards the main road. Away to the left another earthwork is clearly visible and can be easily visited along another path from the track. This a Caer Leb, a settlement of Iron Age origin, surrounded by a double bank and ditch.

At the main road our route crosses straight over and follows a tiny lane leading towards the coast. After about five hundred metres and a left and right turn, a path crosses fields to the left. As it approaches the first buildings another burial chamber can be found in a small field beside the houses. The capstone is large and similar to Bodowyr, but it has collapsed and only one upright is still visible beneath it. Interestingly it is at a similar height and directly opposite the other chamber away across the valley.

The path continues to a lane at the edge of the village and the end of the walk. A Bronze Age round barrow marked on the map on the other side of the village might be worth a visit but was completely hidden beneath crops and a curtain of rain on the only occasion that I searched for it.

This walk gives us only fleeting glimpses of what the valley must have been like in the distant past, and the remaining monuments span at least three thousand years from the early Neolithic to the Roman period. To the Iron Age settlers of Caer Leb the great stones of Tre Dryw must have seemed as unearthly as they do to us. Nevertheless, it shows us a valley steeped in history and offers us at least a shadowy insight into the mysteries of prehistoric Anglesey.

24. Barclodiad y Gawres Rhosneigr

Approx. distance: 7 miles

Approx. time: 4 hours

Starting point: Llanfaelog, GR 337729

Grade: A varied and interesting walk over mostly level lanes and footpaths

O.S. Explorer sheet: 262

Grid references: Barclodiad y Gawres chambered cairn, GR 329707; Ty Newydd burial chamber, GR 344738; Wayside Stores, GR 334726

On the rugged west coast of Anglesey a small promontory juts out into the Irish Sea between the sandy bays of Porth Nobla and Trecastell. On a final grassy knoll, just above where the steep cliffs plunge into the wild waters, is the ancient chambered cairn of Barclodiad y Gawres, 'the giantess's apronful'. Once covered by a huge earthen mound, this much restored but magnificent Neolithic tomb looks out across the sea towards Ireland.

The walk begins in Llanfaelog, where there is ample parking opposite the church. Before you begin it is necessary to visit the Wayside Stores where a key to the burial chamber can be collected for a returnable deposit of £5, and if you have forgotten to bring a torch, one can be purchased for a reasonable price.

From the church it takes the quiet road through Bryn Du, past its two 18th century windmills and over a level crossing beside the tiny station. The quiet lane can then be followed until a farm track branches off to the right towards the farm of Rhosmor. An alternative is to take the track to the remote house at Bryngwyn and then the rather overgrown footpath past a small lake to reach the same place.

In summer these tracks are a swath of colour. Campions and foxgloves line the path, while cranesbill and speedwell twist their way through the tall grasses. And everywhere there are birds. Goldcrests and finches flit along the hedgerows while stonechats perch precariously on thickets of gorse. The reed-fringed waters of the lake teem with waterfowl, and above a shallow valley away to the left buzzards spiral silently upwards on the rising air.

Beyond Rhosmor the track continues to the main road, which is crossed to reach the sandy beach of Porth Trecastell. The waves in this small cove are funnelled in through a narrow mouth and rise into spectacular break-

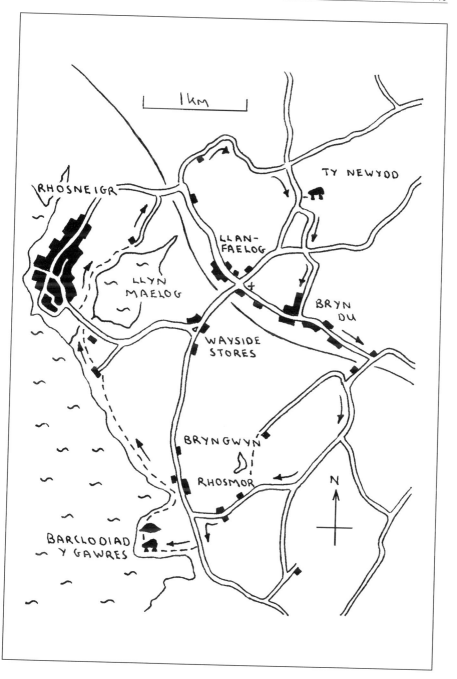

ers, which rip along the rocks of the steep cliffs on either side, making this a most spectacular place.

A path runs along above the cliffs towards the ancient burial cairn on the end of the tiny promontory. This is a lovely section of the walk, across short turf with patches of natural rockery carpeted with thrift and tiny clumps of English stonecrop. Below the path the cliffs are broken into jagged ridges, between which waves crash into narrow zawns (inlets) and tiny rocky coves. The path climbs as it reaches the great cairn, a high grassy dome covering the modern protective shell over the burial chambers.

Using the key, it is possible to enter the semi-darkness of the tomb and experience its unique atmosphere. Without a torch it is still light enough to see the stones lining the 7m long entrance passage leading to a cruciform chamber. Only one of the original capping stones remains, still covering the southern side chamber. The other two side chambers, to the east and west, are uncovered. Fresh offering of flowers, candle stumps and tiny oil lamps stand on some of the stones, as testimony to the continued reverence that this ancient place is held in.

When it was excavated in 1953, the bones of a number of individuals were found in the chambers, along with the burnt and broken remains of pins carved from bone. But it was in the central area that the most amazing discovery was made. It appears that a fire was lit there and kept burning for a long time, and that over it was poured a 'stew' containing the bones of a frog, a toad, a snake, a hare, a mouse and at least three different types of fish. This had then been covered with limpet shells and pebbles. Was this a feast for the dead or some kind of ancient 'witchcraft' whose symbolism now eludes us?

With the aid of a torch it is also possible to look more closely at the stones which line the passage and the two side chambers. Etched into them are many geometric designs. Circles and spirals, lozenges and zigzags decorate the surfaces of at least five of the stones. Seen in the light of a central fire, these must have added greatly to the powerful symbolism of the ceremonies that were held here. Spare a few moments to sit beside the site of the fire and try to imagine the scenes which might have taken place there over 5,000 years ago.

From the cairn the path drops down into a shallow gully leading to a rocky cove, before climbing up to the next rise which was once also crowned with an ancient cairn. Little remains of this except for a low ring of stones about twelve paces across, and the remnants of a stone cist at its centre. The path continues along the top of the rocky shore with fine views to the north-west towards Holyhead Mountain to reach the sandy bay of Porth Nobla.

The inscribed stones of Barclodiad y Gawres

The next section can be done along the beach with its many rocky outcrops or alternatively there is a track that winds its way through the dunes behind. Either way is interesting and pleasant, but for those interested in wild flowers, the dunes offer the chance to find some of the beautiful orchids that can be found there. Through the marram grass, which binds the dunes together, the pink and white flowers of sea bindweed and the deep red patches of bloody cranesbill catch the eye. Much more illusive are the delicate pink cones of the pyramidal orchid which just poke their heads above the rougher vegetation.

At the strange row of houses which stands up above the beach, a path crosses through the dunes and cuts across towards the road with the waters of Llyn Maelog showing clearly beyond. After crossing the stream that flows from the lake, a path leads off to the right, over a small wooden bridge to the lakeside.

The next section is very enjoyable, with tall reedbeds fringing the water and clumps of gorse and wild irises all around. The lake is also a haven for wildlife. On the water, coots and tufted ducks squabble and dive, while overhead long skeins of geese circle around before landing on the far shore. Just beyond a converted chapel, a track turns up from the lake to join a lane, which runs through a campsite and back to the main road.

Turning right, the road passes under a railway bridge, and just before the next sharp bend a quiet lane branches off to the left. For the next mile this lane winds across the low marshy valley of the Afon Crigyll before climbing up onto the rolling farmland beyond. The contrast is fascinating. The open wetland is criss-crossed with dykes, lined with reeds and yellow

Ty Newydd

irises. Oystercatchers and herons are everywhere, and I even once saw a beautiful little egret wading in a shallow pool beside the track. As the lane climbs, hedges and trees increase and gorse and bracken replace the sparser wetland vegetation and the birds of the hedgerow reappear.

Eventually it meets another road at a crossroads and soon after turning right the burial chamber of Ty Newydd appears in a field on the left. The path to it follows a wonderful old walled hedge emblazoned with wild flowers and alive with bees and butterflies.

The dolmen itself is still impressive despite being 'renovated' early in the last century. The great capstone is supported by three original uprights, and because it was splitting, two rather incongruous brick pillars. A fourth upright stands to one side possibly indicating that originally the capstone was much larger even than it appears today. Despite all this, it is an impressive sight and its situation only adds to the atmosphere surrounding it. Sitting in the corner of a quiet field, on a slight rise, there are excellent views away to the hills on the north of the island.

When it was excavated they found a fragment of beaker pottery and a flint arrowhead dating from the Bronze Age within the chamber. However, the size of the chamber, several 'cup marks' on the top of the capstone, and a flake from a polished stone axe suggest that it actually dates back to the early Neolithic period about 5,000 years ago.

Leaving this peaceful spot with great reluctance, it is possible to return quickly along quiet lanes to Bryn Du and Llanfaelog, remembering of course to return the key to the Wayside Stores before setting off for home.

25. Meini Hirion
Cemaes

Approx. distance: 6 miles

Approx. time: 3 hours

Starting point: Llanfechell, GR 369915

Grade: An easy walk along quiet lanes

O.S. Explorer sheet: 262

Grid references: Maeni Hirion, GR 364917; burial chamber, GR 361920; Pen yr orsedd standing stones, GR 334906 and, GR 333904; Llanfechell standing stone, GR 370916

This is a good walk for the late autumn or winter. When the fields are thick with mud and the moors lie sodden beneath a heavy sky, it can be done with dry feet in relative ease and comfort. For the majority of its length it follows quiet lanes through that strange landscape that makes up much of northern Anglesey.

It is a landscape of great contrasts. Crumbling windmills stand against a backdrop of graceful modern wind vanes. Gnarled and ancient trees cling to the slopes of hills through which march lines of pylons from a squat and ugly power station sitting like an obese toad beside the sea. Beautifully preened and landscaped gardens stand beside wild slopes of gorse and splintered rock. Nowhere can it be said to be beautiful, but it remains fascinating for its great diversity.

Largely hidden beneath the thick veneer of more recent times is an almost unnoticed ancient landscape. Standing stones and tumuli are scattered around the low hills, and ancient springs and sacred hills are only recognisable by names that have clung to them stubbornly through the centuries.

The walk starts in Llanfechell. From the northern end of the village a tiny lane runs westwards back towards the main road. After only a hundred metres a footpath turns off to the right, leading between houses and out onto the open fields beyond. Immediately the land begins to rise and up ahead, instantly obvious against the skyline, are the three stones of Meini Hirion, 'the tall stones'.

The path crosses several small fields of open pasture, grazed by wild-looking cattle, to reach them. They stand in a small triangle, each

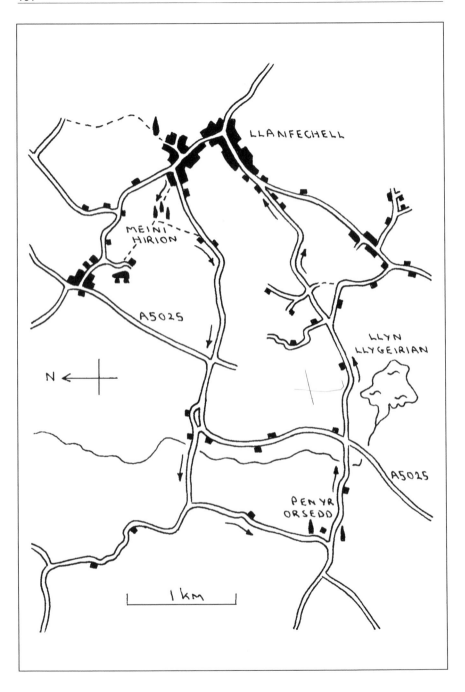

about three paces from the next. Two of them are about eight feet tall and the third only slightly shorter. All of them are very thin and slender, of the same hard metamorphic rock found throughout this part of the island.

Perfectly positioned on the open hilltop, the three stone setting is very unusual. In some parts of western Britain stone circles were eventually reduced to only four stones, but a ring of three is much rarer, and it is the only one still surviving in Wales. Other groups of three stones are set in a line such as Harold's Stones at Trellech near Monmouth. It has been suggested that these represent the three ages of the great goddess, the maiden, the woman and the old hag. The number three must have been a powerful number in ancient times and has since come to be associated with pagan beliefs. The three witches in Macbeth, the granting of three wishes by fairy godmothers and 'third time lucky' are but three of the many examples. It is even possible that the worship of the triple goddess was taken over by Christianity much later when it became converted to the Holy Trinity.

The view from the hilltop is wide and open. Away to the south on the far horizon are the mountains of Snowdonia rising above the low hills of central Anglesey. To the west is the small but dominant hill of Mynydd y Garn and to the north is the sea. Overlying this vast natural and ancient landscape are the works of the modern day. The power lines and the wind farms are not pretty, but they seem only superficial and can never really destroy the underlying beauty of this essentially wild land.

Beyond the stones, in a field beside the next farm are the collapsed and badly damaged remains of a burial chamber, which might once have been associated with the Meini Hirion on the hilltop above.

From the stones, the path up can be easily retraced to the lane, or a short-cut taken down to the left which passes through a farmyard and along a short overgrown track to join the lane slightly further on.

The lane winds along between fields of rough pasture. The old stone walls are almost completely covered in wild tangles of brambles and gorse and stones lie in loose piles where they have been cleared from the fields. As the lane climbs, large rocky outcrops rear up on either side, partly buried beneath thickets of dense scrub. From the top of the rise the view opens out once more. Mynydd y Garn is again prominent, and away to the left the church spire of Llanrhyddlad stands up from the crest of a hill.

The lane drops to the main road, which has to be followed for just a short way, although it can be largely avoided by taking the old road that still runs parallel to it. Another quiet lane turns off beside the ruined windmill, crosses over the stream and heads towards the coast at Cemlyn Bay. After a left turn it is not long before a lone standing stone appears up ahead on the crest of a low rise.

The three stone setting of Meini Hirion

It is huge, all of fifteen feet tall, a great wide blade which seems almost human in shape, like a still and cowled figure against the skyline. The stone is mostly grey but streaked with long vertical lines and starbursts of white quartz. Its top is decorated with a grey-green moss and on the east-facing side are patches of a beautiful, orange lichen. Near its base, the rough rock has been polished smooth and shiny by countless animals rubbing against it over the centuries. It stands in a field, not far from the farm, and can be viewed from the lane, but it is not until you actually stand beneath it that its size and beauty can be fully appreciated.

A second stone stands only a few hundred metres away to the south, again just inside a field beside the lane. Although similar in shape, this one is only about nine feet tall. On its eastern face is a prominent cup mark, a man-made circular hollow carved into the surface, which are quite common on ancient stones but whose purpose is still not fully understood.

On first inspection these two stones seem, like many others in Wales, to be placed at random in the landscape. This was almost certainly not the case, because the effort involved in the quarrying, transporting and erecting of these huge stones would suggest that they were of great significance at the time. This would also mean that their positioning was important.

Cup-marked stone at Pen yr orsedd

Bearing this in mind, it is interesting that the two stones are equidistant from a small hill on which sit the old outbuildings of the farm. The farm is called Pen yr orsedd, literally 'the hilltop of the throne' although throne most likely meant more a place of power or importance than a throne in the modern sense. If a third stone had once stood on the gentle rise in the ground due east of the hillock then together they would have formed a perfect three-point ring around what must have been an important ancient site.

Other examples of standing stones encircling a sacred hill or tomb are rare in Wales but less so in Scotland, and at Hully Hill near Edinburgh there is an almost perfect replica. There, a large but low mound is surrounded at a similar distance by three tall stones also spaced out like the Legs of Man. This is itself a symbol, which dates back to prehistoric times and probably indicates the centre of a circle or wheel about which everything else revolved. Perhaps here in rural Anglesey, now lost beneath the farm, was such a centre of their ancient community.

From Pen yr orsedd the lane winds along, back over the stream and across the main road. Off to the right are the waters of Llyn Llygeirian, fringed with reeds and dotted with wildfowl. Beyond the lake the lane rises gently and the landscape becomes wilder with outcrops of rock and thickets of gorse clothing the hillsides. Away to the south, beyond a tall windmill, are hills crowned with slowly rotating wind vanes and, in the far distance, the high mountains of Snowdonia ring the horizon. To the north, the three stones of Meini Hirion are clearly visible on their hilltop.

The lane eventually drops back into Llanfechell from where the walk began, but an interesting conclusion still lies in wait. Just beyond the last houses on the far side of the village is another huge standing stone. This nine-foot leaning stone is almost as wide as it is tall and why it was placed there remains a mystery. Beyond it is a backdrop of pylons and wind vanes and it seems to typify the strange contrasts of this land. Side by side in this field, stands the new with the old, the useful with the mysterious, modern science beside ancient lore, and strangely, neither seems entirely out of place in this weird and wonderful landscape.

26. Trefignath
Holy Island

Approx. distance: 7 miles

Approx. time: 4 hours

Starting point: Trearddur, GR 255793

Grade: A walk of contrasts – wild coastal paths, quiet country lanes and the urban fringe of Holyhead

O.S. Explorer sheet: 262

Grid references: Iron Age coastal fort, GR 223794; Penrhos Feilw standing stones, GR 227809; Ty Mawr standing stone, GR 254810; Trefignath burial chamber, GR 258806

This really is a walk of contrasts. Like much of Anglesey it bombards the walker and the historian with a range of images which confound and confuse. The scenery is at times magnificent and inspiring, yet at others it is shabby and disappointing with its urban bleakness. Much of the northern end of the once sacred isle of Ynys Gybi, 'Holy Island', has been lost beneath the growth of Holyhead, and the holiday homes which have spread over much of its spectacular coastline. Yet enough still remains unspoilt to make it possible to experience the mystery and magnificence of this historic landscape.

Ancient monuments stand shoulder to shoulder with the monumental works of the 21st century and at first appear insignificant beside the tall towers and urban sprawl of the modern day. But they are not. The town and its factories sit upon the landscape, yet seem not to be a part of it. The roads cut straight through the grain of the land as if unaware of its hills and valleys. The ancient stones and trackways are different. They stand as an integral part of the scenery and seem comfortable within it. They enhance it and pay homage to it. Perhaps this is merely a legacy of the great length of time they have stood within the landscape, but I like to think that it is because their builders felt much more a part of the land on which they lived.

The walk begins in Trearddur, a pleasant town ringed around the beautiful Trearddur Bay. The coast to either side of the small sandy beach rises to low cliffs, which have been sculpted by the waves into rocky islets and tiny coves. At first it follows the road which runs westwards from the town

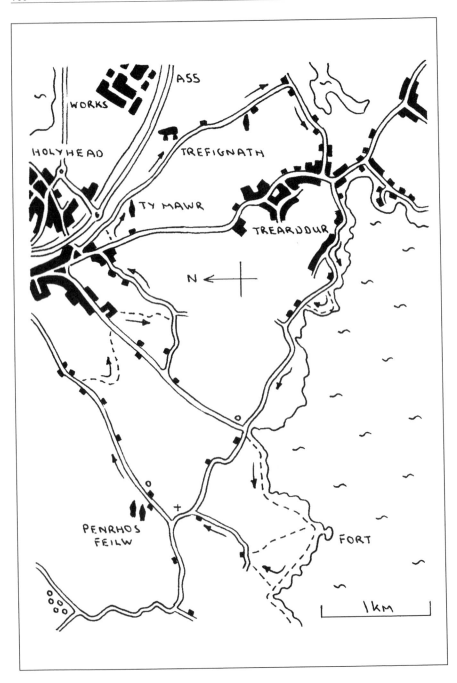

along the edge of the sea. As it comes to the end of the buildings it rises onto a rocky promontory which can be easily scrambled up onto from the road. It is a marvellous viewpoint, cliffs and headlands fading into the distance in both directions.

A short distance further on, a well signposted path allows you to leave the road and wander out along the clifftops to where a small rocky cape is only joined to the mainland by a very narrow and rapidly eroding strip of land. From its tip the sea spreads in an immense arc away to the west, with only the shadowy outline of the Lleyn Peninsula rising from the empty horizon.

The path curls back to rejoin the road, which rises through an area of rocky outcrops and gorse bushes grazed by ponies, before dropping once more to the shore at Porth Dafarch. Ahead, the white dome of Holyhead Mountain dominates the view and in the clear light seems almost close enough to touch. On the slopes of this mountain are the remains of Mesolithic camps where hunters and fishermen lived over 7,000 years ago, and the more obvious hut circles of the Iron Age and the Roman period can still be clearly seen.

Just beside the road above the beach are the jumbled walls and banks of another ancient hut complex, which probably dates from the Iron Age. From there the walk again leaves the road, which turns inland at this point, and after passing a small caravan site, enters a beautiful area of coastal moorland which fringes the rocky coves and steep-sided zawns which slice into the cliffs.

The path picks its way around them and heads towards the end of the headland, which has become virtually separated from the mainland by a great sea-cut chasm up which the waves foam and roar. A spectacular natural arch cuts right through the cliffs at one end. The 'island' beyond can only be gained by a steep and dangerous scramble down to a rocky causeway and another climb up the slopes on the far side. To add to these formidable natural defences, the people of the Iron Age built a banked wall to guard this, the only possible approach.

Having considered but rejected the idea of attempting to reach the fort, it is best to continue along the coastal path to Porth Ruffydd, then turn inland and leave the cries of the gulls behind. This path leads to a lane, which can be quickly followed back to the road. Just beyond the obvious large chapel, a tiny lane turns off to the right, and hidden away behind the first buildings are the stones of Penrhos Feilw.

From the gate into their field, they seem quite small, but as you approach, they grow in stature to become magnificent, ten-foot high blades of Holyhead schist. This wonderful rock is among the most ancient in the

The standing stones of Penrhos Feilw

country, and its wavy grain shines and glistens like oyster shells. The top of each is encrusted with a blue-grey lichen, which seems to emphasise their antiquity. Standing only four paces apart they rise through the low horizon and cut deep into the sky. Framed between them is the rocky hump of Holyhead Mountain.

They probably date from the early Bronze Age and are supposed to have originally stood at the centre of a circle of stones, although no sign of these has survived. It is also said that a stone cist was found between them, which contained spearheads, arrowheads and human bones, but again the evidence for this has long gone. Standing as they do on a crest of a ridge running between low hills, they pay dramatic homage to the holy mountain behind.

From the stones the lane continues for about half a mile until a well-marked footpath turns off to the right. As it climbs over the main spine of the island, the scenery changes dramatically from the rural west to the more developed east. At first the path weaves through a wild area of rocks and gorse, which serves to show just how rugged all of the landscape must once have been. Then it breaks out onto open fields and drops down to a road and the outskirts of Holyhead. Turning left and immediately right into a small 'cul de sac', another path can be taken up over rolling fields before dropping once again to a quiet lane.

At one point it is possible to see an old whitewashed windmill, the tall tower of a modern factory complex and the mountains of Snowdonia all standing one behind the other, yet another example of the strange amalgam of images to be seen on this walk.

The lane is followed past the windmill to a busier road, which is crossed to a footpath leading to another very narrow lane. This runs parallel to the new A55, which fortunately is in a deep cutting and well screened by newly planted trees.

In a field off to the right is a large standing stone known as the Ty Mawr stone. This nine-foot menhir stands on a slight rise in the centre of the field, and is reached by a footpath from the lane. Like the stones of Penrhos Feilw, it dates from the early Bronze Age and is of the same beautifully textured rock.

Further along the lane is the main reason for the walk, the great Neolithic burial chamber of Trefignath. This magnificent monument is, in fact, the product of at least three distinct phases of building spanning almost 1,500 years from about 3,500 BC to 2,000 BC. For it to have remained a feature of their society for such a length of time shows just how significant it must have been to them. Even our oldest churches cannot claim such a period of longevity.

Built onto a natural rocky outcrop, the elevated site commands wide views over the island. The place might well have been an important site even before the first chamber was built, as stone implements and fragments of pottery were found beneath the cairn itself. The original structure was a single box-like tomb covered by a round cairn. At a later date a second chamber was added and the cairn elongated. Finally, the third and best-preserved chamber was built behind two tall portal stones, and covered by a large wedge-shaped cairn. Most of the loose stone has gone, but the chambers remain in varying degrees of repair. That they still stand at all after nearly 6,000 years is a wonder in itself!

It is a peaceful place despite the nearness of the new road and the industrial backdrop of the smelting works just beyond it. Amazingly, the eye is not drawn to these, but away to the north-west, to the white slopes of the Holy Mountain to which the tomb still seems to pay homage.

From Trefignath, it is an easy journey, continuing along the lane and back to Trearddur where the route began.

This is an interesting walk, which visits sites from all periods of early history. Unfortunately, the last century has not been as kind to the Holy

Trefignath

Island as the ones that preceded it, and it is difficult to ignore its many blemishes completely. Despite this, it is rather comforting to feel that the stones of Trefignath and Penrhos Feilw will still crown their rocky knolls long after the great furnaces of the smelting works have been pulled down and consigned to the faded pages of our history books.

Bibliography

Farmers, Temples and Tombs, Gordon Barclay, Canongate Books (1998)

A Guide to the Stone Circles of Britain Ireland and Brittany, Aubrey Burl, Yale (1995)

Circles of Stone, Aubrey Burl, Harvill (1999)

The Snowdonia National Park, W.M. Condry, Collins (1966)

The Modern Antiquarian, Julian Cope, Thorsons (1998)

Standing Stones, Jean-Pierre Mohen, Thames and Hudson (1999)

The Welsh Peaks, W.A. Poucher, Constable (1962)

Prehistoric Art, T.G.E. Powell, Thames and Hudson (1966)

Anglesey, a Guide to the Ancient Monuments, M.J. Yates and David Longley, C.A.D.W. (1989)

Glossary of Technical Terms

Avenue: a ceremonial route lined with paired standing stones, often linking stone circles with places of burial.

Barrow: an earthen mound covering a burial, usually round in shape, and dating from the Bronze Age.

Cairn: a mound of stones, often covering a burial, and usually round in shape.

Cairn circle: a cairn, of which only the kerb stones remain.

Capstone: the stone forming the roof of a burial chamber or cist.

Causewayed camp: a Neolithic enclosure with many entrances which may have been a meeting or market place.

Central stone: single standing stone positioned in the centre of a stone circle.

Chambered cairn: a cairn with a burial chamber, or chambers, inside it.

Cist: a stone sarcophagus usually beneath a cairn or barrow.

Clearance cairn: a cairn made up of stones cleared from land on which crops were raised and not usually associated with burial.

Dolmen : Celtic name for a burial chamber. Literally, a 'stone table'.

Enclosure: an area enclosed with prehistoric banks or ditches.

Forecourt: a stone-lined entrance to a chambered cairn or barrow.

Henge: a circular enclosure surrounded by a bank that sometimes has an interior ditch.

Kerb cairn: a burial cairn where the small cairn stones are held in place by larger kerb stones around the base.

Kerb stones: a ring of larger stones around a cairn, which held in the smaller cairn stones.

Long barrow: a long mound, usually dating from the Neolithic period, usually with burial chambers inside.

Long cairn, or longcairn: a long cairn, usually with burial chambers inside.

Megalith: a large stone, erected or positioned by Man in the Neolithic or Bronze Ages.

Menhir: Celtic name for a standing stone. Literally, a 'tall stone'.

Microliths: Small stone tools and blades, usually made from flakes struck from flint or chert.

Outlier: a standing stone positioned outside a stone circle.

Recumbent: a large circle stone that lies on its side and is sometimes flanked by two tall upright stones. Usually positioned at the south-west section of the circle and often aligned with the horizon. Most commonly found in Aberdeenshire.

Ring cairn, or ringcairn: a ring of cairn stones with a level space inside. Originally they were probably surrounded by a circle of timber posts and were for ceremonial rather than burial purposes.

Standing stone: stones which do not form part of a circle and which may have been waymarkers or portals.

Stone circle: a circular ring of large stones sometimes built into a low bank.

Stone row: a row of stones, often leading to or from a stone circle.

Tumulus: an old name for a barrow.

Glossary of Welsh Place-names

Aber	river mouth	**Dôl**	meadow
Afon	river	**Drosgyl**	rough hill
Allt	wooded slope	**Drum**	high ridge
Aran	high place	**Drws**	door
Arddu	black crag	**Dŵr**	water
		Dyffryn	wide, flat valley
Bach	small		
Bala	outlet	**Eglwys**	church
Bedd	grave	**Eira**	snow
Ber	hilltop	**Esgair**	shoulder of a moun-
Bettws	chapel		tain
Blaen	head of a valley		
Bod	home or house	**Fach**	small
Bont	bridge	**Faes**	field
Brith	speckled	**Fan**	lofty
Bron	slope	**Fawr**	big or large
Bryn	hill	**Felin**	mill
Bwlch	pass or col	**Ffordd**	road
Bychan	small	**Ffynnon**	natural spring or
			well
Cader, Cadair	chair or throne	**Foel**	rounded hill
Cae	field		
Caer	camp or fort	**Gaer**	camp or fort
Canol	middle	**Gallt**	slope
Capel	chapel	**Ganol**	middle
Carn, Carnedd	cairn or mound of	**Garn**	hill
	stones	**Garth**	enclosure
Carreg	stone	**Glas**	blue or green
Castell	castle or fort	**Glider**	pile of stones
Cau	hollow	**Glyn**	deep valley
Cefn	ridge	**Goch**	red
Celli	grove or copse	**Gors**	bog or marsh
Clogwyn	cliff or crag	**Gorsedd**	throne
Clyd	shelter	**Grach**	rough
Coch	red	**Groes**	cross
Coed	wood	**Grug**	heather
Cors	bog or marsh	**Gwastad**	plain or platform
Craig	rock or crag	**Gwern**	swampy thicket
Crib, Cribin	jagged ridge	**Gwyn**	white
Croes	cross	**Gwynt**	wind
Crug	mound		
Cwm	glacial valley	**Hafod**	summer dwelling
		Hagr	rough or wild
Ddu	black	**Hên**	old
Din, Dinas	fort	**Hir**	long or tall

Isaf	lower	**Plas**	important house or place
Llan	church	**Pont**	bridge
Llech	stone	**Pwll**	pool
Lloer	moon		
Llwyd	grey	**Rhaiadr**	waterfall
Llyn	lake	**Rhyd**	ford
Maen	large stone	**Sarn**	causeway or paved track
Maes	field		
Mawr	large	**Sych**	dry
Melyn	yellow		
Mign	bog	**Tomen**	mound
Moel	rounded hill	**Tref**	town
Mynach	monk	**Twll**	hole or cave
Mynydd	mountain	**Tŷ**	house
		Tyddyn	farm
Nant	stream		
Newydd	new	**Uchaf**	upper
Ogof	cave	**Waun**	moor
		Wen	white
Pant	hollow		
Pen	hilltop	**Ynys**	island
Penrhyn	promontory	**Ystrad**	valley floor
Pentre	village	**Ystum**	bend in a river
Pistyll	spout		